TIME TO
GET TOUGH

TIME TO GET TOUGH

MAKING AMERICA #1 AGAIN

BY

DONALD J. TRUMP

Since 1947
REGNERY
PUBLISHING, INC.
An Eagle Publishing Company • Washington, DC

Library of Congress Cataloging-in-Publication Data

Trump, Donald, 1946-
  Time to get tough / by Donald J. Trump.
    p. cm.
  ISBN 978-1-59698-773-9
  1. United States--Economic policy--2009- 2. United States--Economic conditions--2009- 3. United States--Politics and government--2009- I. Title.
  HC106.84.T78 2011
  330.973--dc23
                           2011043852

Published in the United States by
Regnery Publishing, Inc.
One Massachusetts Avenue NW
Washington, DC 20001
www.regnery.com

Manufactured in the United States of America
10 9 8 7 6 5 4 3 2 1

Books are available in quantity for promotional or premium use. Write to Director of Special Sales, Regnery Publishing, Inc., One Massachusetts Avenue NW, Washington, DC 20001, for information on discounts and terms, or call (202) 216-0600.

Distributed to the trade by
Perseus Distribution
387 Park Avenue South
New York, NY 10016

As always,

I dedicate this book to my parents,

Mary and Fred Trump

Contents

ONE

GET TOUGH

Next Tuesday all of you will go to the polls, will stand there in the polling place and make a decision. I think when you make that decision, it might be well if you would ask yourself, are you better off than you were four years ago?

—Ronald Reagan

I've written this book because the country I love is a total economic disaster right now.

For starters, we are in debt $15 trillion and soaring. Let me help you wrap your mind around that number. If by some miracle the so-called leaders in Washington could find a way to save one billion dollars of your tax dollars *every single day*, it would still take thirty-eight years to pay off the debt. And that's not even taking into account the interest.

We don't have thirty-eight years to turn this thing around. The way I see it, we have four, maybe eight years tops.

Every day in business I see America getting ripped off and abused. We have become a laughingstock, the world's whipping boy, blamed for everything, credited for nothing, given no respect. You see and feel it all around you, and so do I.

To take one example, China is bilking us for hundreds of billions of dollars by manipulating and devaluing its currency. Despite all the happy talk in Washington, the Chinese leaders are not our friends. I've been criticized for calling them our enemy. But what else do you call the people who are destroying your children's and grandchildren's future? What name would you prefer me to use for the people who are hell bent on bankrupting our nation, stealing our jobs, who spy on us to steal our technology, who are undermining our currency, and who are ruining our way of life? To my mind, that's an enemy. If we're going to make America number one again, we've got to have a president who knows how to get tough with China, how to out-negotiate the Chinese, and how to keep them from screwing us at every turn.

Then there's the oil crisis. The idea of $85 a barrel for oil used to be unthinkable. Now OPEC yawns at that figure and jacks the price higher, laughing all the way to the bank. The result: you and your family are paying $3 a gallon, $4 a gallon, $5 a gallon, and soaring. Excuse me, but OPEC—these twelve guys sitting around a table—wouldn't even be in existence if it weren't for the United States saving and protecting those Middle Eastern countries! Where is our president in all this? Where's the accountability? What is the point of executive leadership if our executive is weak and doesn't lead? What excuse is there for a president whose answer to the oil crisis is not to get tough with OPEC, not to free our own domestic oil companies to do their job and drill, but to release our strategic reserve? That's not leadership, that's an abdication of leadership.

Whether we like it or not, oil is the axis on which the world's economies spin. It just is. When the price of oil goes up, so does the price of just about everything else. Think about it. You buy a loaf of bread. How did it get to the store? What powered the bread truck? What equipment did the farmer use to harvest the grain? Equipment and vehicles don't fuel themselves. They need oil. And when a producer's prices go up, they pass the cost along to you in the form of higher prices. I was privileged to be educated at the finest business school in the world, the Wharton School of Business. But it doesn't take some prestigious business diploma to realize what's going on here. It's basic math.

And yet, with China beating us like a punching bag daily, OPEC vacuuming our wallets clean, and jobs nowhere in sight, what does President Obama do? He makes his NCAA basketball picks. He hosts lavish parties at the White House. Now look, I like basketball and lavish parties like the next person. But when you're the president of the United States and your country is burning to the ground right before your eyes, your first instinct should not be to party. It's no wonder America is flat broke.

Did you know that one in seven Americans is now on food stamps?[1] Think of it. In the United States, the most prosperous nation in the history of human civilization, our people are going hungry. In March 2011, we saw the steepest spike in food prices in almost four decades.[2] Combine that with skyrocketing energy costs, double-digit unemployment, Obama's massively wasteful spending spree, the federal government's annexation of the health-care system, and the outcome is painfully clear—we're headed for economic disaster. If we keep on this path, if we reelect Barack Obama, the America we leave our kids and grandkids won't look like the America we were blessed to grow up in. The American Dream will be in hock. The shining city on the hill will start to look like an inner-city wreck. It won't be morning in America, as President Reagan put it. We'll be *mourning for* America, an America that was lost on Obama's watch. The dollar will fall as the world's international currency. Our economy will collapse again (something I believe is a very real danger and risk: a double dip recession that could turn into a depression). And China will replace America as the world's number one economic power.

But it doesn't have to be this way. If we get tough and make the hard choices, we can make America a rich nation—and respected—once again. The right president can actually make America money by brokering big deals. We don't always think of our presidents as jobs and business negotiators, but they are. Presidents are our dealmakers in chief. But the outcome of a deal is only as effective as the person brokering it. Constitutionally, a president is the commander in chief, appoints judges, and can veto or sign bills. What's his job the rest of the time? Well, I can tell you one important job: he serves as America's chief negotiator and dealmaker. He is supposed to broker deals that protect and benefit us with other nations. The president's duty is to create an environment where free and fair markets can flourish, private sector jobs can be created, and our economy can boom. If they are strong negotiators and make the right deals,

America wins. If they wimp out and make the wrong deals, you and your children pay the price.

Now consider the embarrassing and anemic deals Obama has pulled off. I'm for free and fair trade. After all, I do business all over the world. But look at the deal Obama cut with South Korea. It was so bad, so embarrassing, that you can hardly believe anyone would sign such a thing. In theory, the agreement was supposed to boost American exports to South Korea. In reality, the agreement Obama signed will do next to nothing to even out the trade imbalance, will further erode American manufacturing and kill more American jobs, and will wipe away the tariffs South Korea presently pays us to sell their stuff in our country. Why would Obama agree to these terms, especially when we hold all the cards? The South Koreans like our military defending them against North Korea. But they don't need us to do their dirty work—South Korea's armed forces number between 600,000 and 700,000. And yet we still have 28,500 American troops in South Korea.[3] Why?

Even if you think it's a good idea for us to keep troops in South Korea, why isn't South Korea footing the whole bill for our defending them? (Currently they only cover a portion of the costs.) Better still, why is our president signing the trade bill that the South Koreans want him to sign instead of the one that gives *us* maximum advantage? He may have been a good "community organizer," but the man is a lousy international dealmaker. This is hardly a surprise—he's never built or run a business in his life. His entire career of dealmaking, such as it is, has been finding ways for government to shakedown taxpayers to reward his special interest groups. That's not the kind of dealmaker we need.

Then look at China. There are four Chinese people for every American. China's population is massive, and its economic power is huge and growing. China is now the second-largest economy in the world. We are building China's wealth by buying all their products, *even though we make better products in America.* I know. I buy a lot of products. Windows, sheet rock, you name it, I buy it by the truckload. I buy American whenever I can. Unfortunately, a lot of times American businesses can't buy American products because, with the Chinese screwing around with their currency rates, American manufacturers can't be competitive on price. If China didn't play games with its currency and we played on a level economic playing field, we could easily out-compete China. But the Chinese cheat with currency manipulation and with industrial espionage—and our alleged commander in chief *lets them cheat.* The whole thing is a scandal and unfair to our workers and businesses. There's no way America can become rich again if we continue down the path we're on.

Yet with all this, in January 2011, Barack Obama kowtowed to China's president Hu Jintao and welcomed him to the White House. He even gave the Communist leader the high honor of an official State Dinner. China's economy enjoys double-digit growth at our expense, while China screws us with every turn of its currency, is the biggest commercial espionage threat we face, continues its deplorable human rights abuses, and Obama's response is to roll out the red carpet? It's incompetence that borders on betrayal.

Obama legitimized China on the world stage. So what did he get in return? Export deals amounting to a measly $45 billion. Obama's team immediately declared him a master negotiator. In 2009, our trade deficit with China was nearly $230 billion. A pathetic $45 billion in trade contracts is an insulting joke. But when Hu Jintao looks across the negotiating table, he sees the kind of spinelessness and amateurism that lets him know he can buy us off by whisking a few crumbs our way. I believe America's honor shouldn't be for sale. We shouldn't entertain Communists and beg for a few tiny contracts. Instead, a true commander in chief would sit down with the Chinese and demand a real deal, a far better deal. Either China plays by the rules or we slap tariffs on Chinese goods. End of story. This year, by the way, our deficit with China will be more that $350 billion—they are laughing at us.

I love America. And when you love something, you protect it passionately—fiercely, even. We are the greatest country the world has ever known. I make no apologies for this country, my pride in it, or my desire to see us become strong and rich again. After all, wealth funds our freedom. But for too long we've been pushed around, used by other countries, and ill-served by politicians in Washington who measure their success by how rapidly they can expand the federal debt, and your tax burden, with their favorite government programs.

America can do better. I think we deserve the best. That's why I decided to write this book. The decisions we face are too monumental, too consequential, to just let slide. I have answers for the problems that confront us. I know how to make America rich again. I've built businesses across the globe. I've dealt with foreign leaders. I've created tens of thousands of American jobs. My whole life has been about executing deals and making real money—massive money. That's what I do for a living: make big things happen, and now I am worth more than $7 billion.

Restoring American wealth will require that we get tough. The next president must understand that America's business is business. We need a president who knows how to get things done, who can keep America strong, safe, and free, and who can negotiate deals that benefit America, not the countries on the other side of the table. A president doesn't "create" jobs, only businesses can do that. But he can help create an environment that allows the rest of us—entrepreneurs, small businessmen, big businessmen—to make America rich.

The damage that Democrats, weak Republicans, and this disaster of a president have inflicted on America has put us in a mess like we've never seen before in our lifetimes. To fix the problem we've got to be smart and get tough. There's no time to waste.

TWO

TAKE THE OIL

If you put the federal government in charge of the
Sahara Desert, in five years there'd be a shortage of sand.

—**Milton Friedman**

When you do someone a favor, they say thank you. When you give someone a loan, they pay you back. And when a nation like the United States sacrifices thousands of lives of its own young servicemen and women and more than a trillion dollars to bring freedom to the people of Iraq, the least—the absolute *least*—the Iraqis should do is pick up the tab for their own liberation.

How much is it worth to them to be rid of the bloodthirsty dictatorship of Saddam Hussein and to have gained a democracy in which they can vote and have a freely elected parliament? In reality, that's a priceless gift, although after being blown to pieces, many people think that they were better off before. When I say they should pay us back, I'm not even talking about cash out of their pockets. All I'm asking is that they give us, temporarily, a few flows of oil—enough to help pay us back and help take care of the tens of thousands of families and children whose brave loved ones died or were injured while securing Iraqi freedom.

But does Iraq do that? No. In fact, they've made it clear they have no intention of doing so. Ever.

To the Victor Go the Spoils

In June 2011, Republican Congressman Dana Rohrabacher of California visited Iraq and told Iraqi Prime Minister Nouri al-Maliki that he hoped Iraq would someday consider repaying America for all our sacrifices on Iraq's behalf. The Prime Minister's response was to have his press spokesman, Ali al-Dabbagh, call up the U.S. embassy and say that they wanted the congressman to get out of their country and that his remarks were "inappropriate."

Excuse me? Inappropriate? What's "inappropriate" is the fact that America puts up with this garbage. We've spent blood and treasure defending the people of the Middle East, from Iraq to Kuwait to Saudi Arabia and the small Gulf states. And if any country in the Middle East won't sell us their oil at a fair market price—oil that we discovered, we pumped, and we made profitable for the countries of the Middle East in the first place—we have every right to take it.

The ingratitude of Iraq's leadership is breathtaking. This year, the Baghdad city government even had the audacity to demand that America pay $1 billion for the aesthetic damage caused by blast walls we erected to protect the people of Baghdad from bombs. That's like a drowning man charging a lifeguard for having torn his swimsuit in the process of saving his life.

Granted, eight years ago when we were told that we would be greeted in the streets by the Iraqi people with flowers and welcomed as liberators, I didn't buy it. But as far as I'm concerned, Iraq can keep its flowers—the oil is a different matter. We should take the oil. And here's why: because the Iraqis won't be able to keep it themselves. Their military, even as we try to rebuild it, is incompetent, and the minute we leave, Iran will take over Iraq and its great oil reserves, the second largest after Saudi Arabia. If that happens, all of our brave men and women will have died in vain and $1.5 trillion will have been squandered.

So, if Iran is going to take over the oil, I say *we* take over the oil first by hammering out a cost-sharing plan with Iraq. If we protect and control the oil fields, Iraq will get to keep a good percentage of its oil—not to mention its independence from Iran—and we will recoup some of the cost of liberating the Iraqis and also pay back the nations that fought with us in the war. And I want to repay the families of the soldiers who died or were terribly wounded. Of course, nothing can ever replace a lost life or a lost limb, but we can send the children of dead or badly wounded veterans to college, provide compensation to the spouses of our service members killed in Iraq, and make sure that wounded veterans are properly looked after. It's common sense, and peanuts compared to what is lying under Iraq's land. Each American family who lost a loved one in Iraq should be given $5 million, and our wounded veterans should be given money, perhaps $2 million each plus medical costs.

Call me old school, but I believe in the old warrior's credo that "to the victor go the spoils." In other words, we don't fight a war, hand over the keys to people who hate us, and leave. We win a war, take the oil to repay the financial costs we've incurred, and in so doing, treat Iraq and everybody else fairly. As General Douglas MacArthur said, "There is no substitute for victory." From the very beginning of Operation Iraqi Freedom, I believed we should have hammered out the repayment plan with the Iraqis—through exiled Iraqi dissidents—*before* we launched the war and rid the people of Iraq of their murderous dictator, Saddam Hussein. And back then, there were a few smart people who agreed with me and said the same thing. One of them was the director of the Defense Department's Office of Net Assessment, Andrew Marshall. He recommended that oil revenues should be used to reduce the sticker price for occupation.[1] Of course, that hasn't happened. Still, there's no reason we can't or shouldn't implement a cost-sharing arrangement with Iraq. Do not take no for an answer.

It's hardly a radical idea. In September 2010, our own Government Accountability Office (GAO) and others studied the issue in depth and concluded that a cost-sharing plan is feasible and wise. All the know-nothings in the White House need to do is read the cover of the report: "Iraqi-U.S. Cost-Sharing: Iraq Has a Cumulative Budget Surplus, Offering the Potential for Further Cost-Sharing." That's literally the title. And if they actually read the first line of the report, they would know the GAO found that the Iraqi government is running a budget *surplus* of $52.1 billion.[2] Iraq just came through a lengthy war and they're already back in business and flush with cash. Why are we footing the bill and getting nothing in return?

I'll give you the answer. It's because our so-called "leaders" in Washington know absolutely nothing about negotiation and dealmaking. Look, I do deals—big deals—all the time. I know and work with all the toughest operators in the world of high-stakes global finance. These are hard-driving, vicious, cutthroat financial killers, the kind of people who leave blood all over the boardroom table and fight to the bitter end to gain maximum advantage. And guess what? Those are *exactly* the kind of negotiators the United States needs, not these cream puff "diplomats" Obama sends around the globe to play patty cake with foreign governments. No, we need smart people with titanium spines and big brains who love America enough to fight fiercely for our interests. Ronald Reagan's Secretary of State George Shultz used to ask diplomats into his office and, standing before a map, ask them what country they represented. When they pointed to their assigned country, he'd correct them and say, "No, that's not your country, you represent the United States." Leadership starts with the person at the top. The president sets the tone. Ronald Reagan put America first, and he knew how to negotiate. Barack Obama is no Ronald Reagan—not even close. And that's why we're in the mess we're in and why our nation is on the wrong track and doing so badly.

Until we get a new president, our congressmen will continue to be treated with contempt by the Iraqi government, that government will continue to run a surplus at our expense, and we will continue to suffer economically because the Iraqi government, and everyone else, knows

Obama is weak and won't stand up for America's interests. The man's natural instinct is to bow before every foreign leader he can find.

We don't owe the Middle East any apologies. America is *not* what's wrong with the world. We're an example of freedom to the world. No one can match America. We have big hearts—and the courage to do what's right. But we're not the world's policemen. And if we have to take on that role, we need to send a clear message that protection comes at a price. If other countries benefit from our armed forces protecting them, those countries should cover the costs. Period.

Leadership Is Down, Gas Prices Are Up

Beyond simple justice, and beyond reducing our national debt, another advantage of taking the oil is that it will significantly bring down the price of gas. Gas prices are crippling our economy. In the first two years of the Obama administration, gas prices leapt a shocking 104 percent. That's hardly the "hope and change" Americans voted for. That said, there are many environmentalists who are cheering and applauding higher prices. Their logic, if you can call it that, is that if we drive less we will emit less carbon, which will allegedly help alleviate the make-believe problem of global warming. Don't forget, when he was a United States senator, Obama himself suggested that higher gas prices would be a good thing, but that he would prefer a "gradual adjustment."[3]

Then look at the person Obama appoints as his Energy Secretary— Steven Chu, a guy who actually told the *Wall Street Journal*, "Somehow we have to figure out how to boost the price of gasoline to the levels in Europe."[4] So the fact that we've seen a 104 percent jump in the price of a gallon of gas since Obama was elected president should hardly come as a surprise to anyone who was paying attention. He and his supporters telegraphed as much all along. As crazy as it sounds, these folks want higher energy prices because they believe that will force Americans to drive less and businesses to slow down on production and transportation, which they think is a good thing, but which in fact will only cost us more jobs and put us at a greater economic disadvantage against China. Whose side are they on, anyway?

Here's another one: Cap and Tax (or as they called it, Cap and Trade). Remember that? When he was campaigning to become president, Obama outright admitted that his plan to tax businesses on carbon emissions that exceeded his arbitrary cap would drive energy prices sky high. Here's exactly what he said:

> Under my plan of a cap and trade system, electricity rates would necessarily skyrocket, even regardless of what I say about whether coal is good or bad, because I'm capping greenhouse gases, coal-powered plants, you know, natural gas, you name it. Whatever the plants were, whatever the industry was, they would have to, uh, retrofit their operations. That will cost money. They will pass that money on to consumers.[5]

Most of us shake our heads in disbelief at this stuff. But you really have to understand the fringe Left's radical mindset and just how extreme and out of touch with reality this president and his dwindling group of supporters are with the rest of the country. They *want* us to have higher energy prices, they *want* to deprive our economy of the fuel it needs to grow, they *intentionally* put the pseudo-science of global warming and socialist management of our economy—the two go together—ahead of making our economy competitive and creating real private sector jobs for the American people.

The fact is, you're not going to see real growth or create real jobs until we get these exorbitant energy costs under control. Someone needs to tell this president that business owners are not the enemy; they're the people who create jobs. Government can't create jobs. All it can do is put more people on the taxpayer's dime. All it can do is sap our nation's wealth.

The real way to help the 14.4 million unemployed Americans get their jobs back is not through "stimulus spending" that only has you, the tax-payer, cutting the check for yet more government employees. The real way is limiting taxes, slashing crippling and unnecessary regulations, and keeping commodity and fuel costs low.

If our "community organizer in chief" would take the time to study the marketplace, he would know that over the past year, things like fruit, pasta, coffee, bacon, and lots of other foods have registered price spikes as high as 40 percent, and there's no end in sight—in large part because of the price of oil, which has spiked transportation and fertilizer costs.[6] Until we get this country's lifeblood—oil—back down to reasonable rates, America's economy will continue to slump, jobs won't get created, and American consumers will face ever-rising prices.

We can talk all day about windmills, nuclear power, and solar, geo-thermal, and other alternative fuels. I'm all for developing alternatives to oil, but that's for the long term. The fact is, right now and for the foreseeable future, the planet runs on oil—and that means we need to get the price of a barrel of oil down—way down, maybe even to $20 a barrel—and boy would our economy rock.

Does Obama do that? No. He goes around the country lecturing everyone that they need to buy hybrid vehicles, before hopping in his carbon-spewing presidential limousine and Air Force One. If he's really concerned about carbon emissions and air pollution, then maybe he should have grounded his wife before she jetted off with forty of her "closest friends" on a lavish vacation to Spain on the taxpayers' dime. I've got a private jet and love taking my wife and kids on expensive trips too, but there are two differences: I pay for it myself, and I don't go around waving my finger in people's faces lecturing them on the evils of travel and restricting their economic freedoms.

Obama promised he was going to create millions of so-called "green collar" jobs. He used that promise to justify his massive government giveaway of billions and billions of taxpayers' dollars to green energy companies. We're now seeing the results of Obama's promise and big government scheme. Solyndra, a U.S. solar panel company, turned out to be a total bust. They were selling $6 solar panels for $3. It doesn't take a genius to realize that's a loser of a business model. But Solyndra's owner, billionaire George Kaiser, had an inside connection with Obama: Kaiser was a big Obama donor and one of the president's campaign fundraiser "bundlers." So the Obama administration fast-tracked a $535 million federally guaranteed loan. Obama believed so much in Kaiser and Solyndra that he made a big public relations event at Solyndra to deliver a speech singing the praises of Solyndra, green jobs, and justifying why taxpayers should foot the bill to stimulate green companies. Predictably, the company went bankrupt, its 1,100 workers lost their jobs, and the American taxpayer got the shaft, to the tune of over half a billion dollars.

Obama has played off the Solyndra scandal, saying he has no regrets and that the company "went through the regular review process."[7] However, in the wake of FBI investigations, the truth is now leaking out. According to the *Washington Post*, emails have now been released revealing that "evidence is mounting that there was something irregular about the way the Solyndra deal got greenlighted."[8] I predict that there will be many more "Solyndra-style" revelations in the months to come. But Solyndra just shows you that this bunch is engaged in the very crony capitalism and insider deal-cutting that they are always accusing others of. Worse, it shows that the millions of green jobs Obama promised were completely bogus.

But even more shocking than the hypocrisy of it all is the total cluelessness it reveals. At one of the president's speaking events, a man told Obama that he and his wife need a bigger vehicle because they have eight kids. So what did Obama do? He told the guy, "Buy a hybrid van." Just one problem: *they don't exist in America*. This president cannot even speak intelligently without a teleprompter. It's embarrassing and sad!

When he's not hectoring people about hybrids, he's appointing his Attorney General Eric Holder to conduct criminal investigations of gas stations engaging in "price gouging." This is a silly attempt to scapegoat and deflect attention away from how ineffective and weak he is on energy policy. As anyone with a brain knows, the reason gas prices are through the roof is because OPEC controls supply and therefore massively inflates crude oil prices.[9]

America doesn't have time for games. This country is in huge trouble. It's time to get serious and look at the facts. Currently, we're paying over $85 a barrel for oil. The United States uses about 7 billion barrels of oil a year. Do the math. We're singlehandedly transferring hundreds of billions of dollars a year to OPEC countries that hate our guts. And again, we're giving all this money to governments who seethe with anti-American hatred. It's stupid policy.

Take On the Oil Thugs

With proper leadership, we can get that price down to $40–$50 a barrel, if not the $20 that I have previously suggested. But to get there we need a president who will get tough with the real price gougers—not your local gas station, but the illegal cartel that's holding American wealth hostage, OPEC. OPEC stands for the Organization of the Petroleum Exporting Countries. It was created at the Baghdad Conference in September 1960 by our good buddies Iran, Venezuela, Saudi Arabia, Iraq, and Kuwait. Since then OPEC has added as members Angola, Ecuador, Qatar, Algeria, the United Arab Emirates, Nigeria, and our dear friend Libya. So here you have twelve men (in this case they're all men) sitting around a table determining and fixing the price of oil. Now, if you have a store and I have a store and we collude to set prices, we go to jail. But that's what these guys do, and no one lifts a finger. And the worst part of it is that these twelve OPEC countries control 80 percent of the world's accessible oil.[10]

Let your eyes dart back up to that list of OPEC's founding members. First up, Iran. Iranian President Mahmoud Ahmadinejad has called for wiping our close ally Israel off the map. He said that the September 11 terrorist attacks on New York were a plot by the United States government. He believes the Holocaust is a "myth." His regime is developing nuclear weapons in violation of the Nuclear Non-Proliferation Treaty. Next, Hugo Chavez's Venezuela. During one of his rambling United Nations speeches, Chavez called President George W. Bush "the devil." His mouthpiece in Venezuela, ViVe TV, issued a press release in January 2010, saying the 200,000 innocent victims of the awful Haiti earthquake were really killed by an American "earthquake weapon."[11] Then look at Saudi Arabia. It is the world's biggest funder of terrorism.[12] Saudi Arabia funnels our petro dollars—our very own money—to fund the terrorists that seek to destroy our people, while the Saudis rely on us to protect them! Then there is Kuwait, which would not even exist had we and our allies not fought the First Gulf War against Saddam's aggression. And of course we have Iraq, whose freedom we've paid for to the tune of more than a trillion dollars and more than 4,000 dead servicemen and women. These countries do us no favors. Through OPEC they squeeze us for every penny they can get out of us.

Two years ago, Amy Myers Jaffe, an energy expert from the James A. Baker III Institute for Public Policy at Rice University, did a study to determine the real product cost of a barrel of oil. The price of a barrel of oil back then was $60. Jaffe found that the actual cost to produce a barrel of oil then was $15, exactly a quarter of the actual market price.[13] That means you're looking at a 400 percent markup on pricing before the oil even gets to the refinery to be turned into gas. Again, if you or I did this, we would be thrown in jail, because it's illegal to collude and fix prices. But these petro thugs do this year in and year out and laugh all the way to the bank. They claim they're not restricting oil production to jack up the prices, but that's a lie. In 1973, OPEC produced 30 million barrels a day. Guess how much they produced in 2011? That's right, the same amount. Production hasn't moved an inch. The reason for this is *not* because OPEC countries have reached peak oil output. After all, as Robert Zubin points out, as recently as April 2011, the Saudis announced they were going to cut production by 800,000 barrels a day, so they're nowhere near running at full capacity.[14] Instead, OPEC is squeezing production so oil prices skyrocket and America pays.

The OPEC countries wouldn't even exist if it weren't for us—it's our money that makes them rich and our troops that have made Iraq free and kept Kuwait, Qatar, and Saudi Arabia from being gobbled up by Saddam Hussein (or now, potentially, by Iran). A smart negotiator would use the leverage of our dollars, our laws, and our armed forces to get a better deal from OPEC. It's time to get tough. And smart!

Sue OPEC

We can start by suing OPEC for violating antitrust laws.

Currently, bringing a lawsuit against OPEC is difficult. It's been made even more complicated by a 2002 federal court, and subsequent appeals courts, ruling that "under the current state of our federal laws the individual member states of OPEC are afforded immunity from suit brought for damage caused by their commercial activities when they act through OPEC."[15] The way to fix this is to make sure that Congress passes and the president signs the "No Oil Producing and Exporting Cartels Act" (NOPEC) (S.394), which will amend the Sherman Antitrust Act and make it illegal for any foreign governments to act collectively to limit production or set prices. If we get it passed, the bill would clear the way for the United States to sue member nations of OPEC for price-fixing and anti-competitive behavior.

One of the smart people in this debate is Iowa Republican Senator Chuck Grassley, a co-sponsor of the bill. "It's time to get it passed," says Grassley. "OPEC needs to know we are committed to stopping anti-competitive behavior."

Here's the good news: since 2000, this bill has passed the Senate Judiciary Committee four times with bipartisan support, and in May 2008, the NOPEC bill passed in the House when Democrats were in control. Now the bad news: President George W. Bush got spooked and threatened to veto the bill because he was afraid that, with the wars in Iraq and Afghanistan raging, NOPEC might spark "retaliatory action." Bush's fear was misguided. First of all, these oil shakedown artists need and want our money. What are they going to do? Fold their arms, throw a temper tantrum, and refuse to sell us their oil and be out billions and billions of dollars? Give me a break. And two, they *already* engage in "retaliatory action": it's called a 104 percent spike in the price of gas since Obama took office, and that's with him going around practically kissing their feet.

Thomas W. Evans was an adviser to Presidents George H. W. Bush and Ronald Reagan. Evans says that when OPEC or its member nations realize the likelihood of the huge damages they would face and how their illegal actions would be curtailed, they would be forced to seek a settlement on production goals that would put prices in much closer alignment with actual costs. The net effect, says Evans, would be price reductions for heating fuel and gas at the pump that would be so large they might exceed the $168 billion the government spent on the 2008 federal stimulus package. As for concern over any potential fallout, he says what I say: getting tough is getting smart. Suing OPEC "would undoubtedly anger political leaders in the Middle East," writes Evans. "But how stable is the Middle East right now? And isn't starting a lawsuit better than starting a war?"[16]

Imagine how much money the average American would save if we busted the OPEC cartel. Imagine how much stronger economic shape we would be in if we made the Iraqi government agree to a cost-sharing plan that paid us back the $1.5 trillion we've dropped on liberating Iraq so it could have a democratic government. Just those two acts of leadership alone would represent a huge leap forward for our country. And by the way, it would also make us respected again in the world. It's sad—truly sad and disgraceful—the way Obama has allowed America to be abused and kicked around. All we have to do is be smart and show some backbone to begin setting things right.

Use America's Resources and Create Jobs

So number one, we take the oil through the cost-sharing plans that even the GAO says are smart and feasible. Two, we hit OPEC in the wallet and rein them in by signing into law the bipartisan NOPEC law. And the third thing we need to do is to take advantage of one of our country's chief assets—natural gas. We are the "Saudi Arabia" of natural gas, but we don't use it. Abu Dhabi recently had all of their transportation converted to natural gas so they can sell their expensive oil to us.[17] Even they recognize how efficient natural gas is. It's cleaner, cheaper, and better. So why aren't we using it to our advantage?

Did you know that with the natural gas reserves we have in the United States we could power America's energy needs for the next 110 years? Those aren't my estimations, that's what the United States Energy Department's Energy Information Administration says. In fact, one of the larger mother lodes of natural gas, the Marcellus Shale, could produce the energy equivalent of 87 billion barrels of oil.[18] Some critics believe those numbers might be inflated. Fine. Let's say the real number is fifty-five years of energy, or that we only get 43 billion barrels' worth of energy. So what? That buys us more time to innovate and develop newer, more efficient, cleaner, and cheaper forms of energy.

The point is that sitting around handwringing all day accomplishes nothing. Yes, I want us to extract the shale gas safely and responsibly. Who doesn't? But too often, environmental extremists take things so far that they will never be pleased. They're for nuclear energy, then they're against it. They like natural gas, then they don't like it because of new drilling techniques. They want windmills everywhere, then they oppose them because they hack birds to pieces and create "visual pollution" (about this, I agree!). They love ethanol, then they don't anymore because it eats up vast amounts of farm land and sparks food riots in Africa when the price of corn goes up. They like electric cars, then they don't because they realize that half of electricity comes from coal, and they hate coal. On and on, back and forth it goes. Meanwhile, our country's economy is sinking like a stone.

What people need to know is what the great conservative economist and writer Thomas Sowell taught us: in the world of economics, there are no such things as "solutions," only tradeoffs. Every action has a consequence. Every decision has an upside and a downside. So you make smart decisions that minimize harm and maximize freedom. One of the many reasons why I'm a conservative is because I believe in the so-called Law of Unintended Consequences—the idea that, no matter how good government's intentions, when you start social engineering or messing around with the free market, more often than not you open a Pandora's box of negatives you didn't see coming.

So, in terms of energy, we need to be exploring and developing numerous approaches... and I also include in that drilling for oil right here at home. We have oil all over the place in America. It's incredible how much oil is right under our own land and water. But the Obama administration refuses to get tough with the environmental lobby and liberate our oil companies to drill for domestic oil.

Yes, the BP oil spill was bad, but it was no reason to put tighter clamps on domestic drilling. That showed no leadership at all. What it showed was that the Obama administration is driven more by hysteria than facts.

You want some facts? Here's one that anyone who has ever studied oceanic oil supplies already knows: "Tens of millions of gallons of crude oil leak into the ocean every day. Naturally, from the sea floor," as David Ropeik from Harvard University, hardly a rightwing institution, has written.[19] I also read from the U.S. National Academy of Sciences that the ocean itself is to blame for contributing "the highest amount of oil to the marine environment."[20] So if the extreme environmental crazies have a beef to pick with anyone, perhaps it should be with Mother Earth herself.

The real issue, of course, is that those who oppose drilling in the United States simply don't want the drilling to occur in their own backyard. What they ignore is the fact that the holes are going to get drilled into the planet anyway. We should drill them on our soil and create our own jobs and keep the revenue here instead of exporting it to the Middle East. Remember when Obama gave his 2008 speech at the Democratic National Convention and said that he would "invest" $150 billion in renewable energy over the next ten years and create "five million new jobs?" How did that turn out? He spent $80 billion of your and my money and, by his own Council of Economic Advisors' admission, "created or saved" just 225,000 jobs. Now run those numbers: that's $335,000 for each so-called "green collar" job we created or "saved," whatever that means.[21]

Sadly, when it comes to using the energy industry to create American jobs, Obama has been a total disaster. And that's a shame, because he's missing a huge opportunity that could give a lot of people good quality jobs while helping get our country back on solid economic footing. Just look at how he's mismanaged offshore oil drilling. Here at home, he's kept in place the bans on drilling off our coasts. But he goes to Brazil, gives them $2 billion through the U.S. Export-Import Bank, and *brags* that he's proud and excited to make America one of Brazil's "best customers." Pull it up on YouTube and watch it for yourself, if you can stomach it. It's the most ludicrous, anemic leadership anyone could imagine. Think about it. If Obama supports offshore drilling in Brazil, and puts billions of *our* dollars in *their* hands to do it, why can't we drill in America and create more jobs and less dependence on foreign sources of oil?

The fact that Obama decided to tap into our nation's Strategic Petroleum Reserve—a stockpile of 727 million barrels of emergency oil, or thirty-four days' worth of America's annual usage—and used up 30 million barrels to lower summertime gas prices so he could goose his sinking approval ratings is a national disgrace. But ironically, his decision only proves what everyone knows: more domestically produced oil on the market will drive down gas prices. Period.

So let's drill already. And let's do it in America. It's not only economically smart, it's strategic—the Middle East needs to get the message loud and clear that we're done coming to them on bended knee. We're waking up, getting up, and making America the powerhouse we once were.

Take the oil, sue OPEC, and drill domestically—if we do these three big things, we'll be on the right track to rebuild American strength, wealth, jobs, and opportunity. Will it be tough? Sure. But that's what makes us Americans: we do hard things, and we do them well . . . if we have the right leadership.

THREE

TAX CHINA TO SAVE AMERICAN JOBS

*Increasingly, the center of gravity in this world
is shifting to Asia.*[1]

—**Barack Obama**

W hen it comes to China, Barack Obama practices "pretty please" diplomacy. He begs and pleads and bows—and it's been a colossal failure.

Get it straight: China is not our friend. They see us as the enemy. Washington better wake up fast, because China is stealing our jobs, sending a wrecking ball through our manufacturing industry, and ripping off our technology and military capabilities at Mach speed. If America doesn't get wise soon, the damage will be irreversible.

There is a lot that Obama and his globalist pals don't want you to know about China's strength. But no one who knows the truth can sit back and ignore how dangerous this economic powerhouse will be if our so-called leaders in Washington don't get their acts together and start standing up for American jobs and stop outsourcing them to China. It's been predicted that by 2027, China will overtake the United States as the world's biggest economy—much sooner if the Obama economy's disastrous trends continue.[2] That means in a handful of years, America will be engulfed by the economic tsunami that is the People's Republic of China—my guess is by 2016 if we don't act fast.

This didn't happen overnight or in a vacuum. We've been kicking the can down the road and ignoring the warning signs for years. Truth be told, we took a strong jobs beating from China during President George W. Bush's term. Even before the Obama-led employment disaster we're stuck in now, from 2001 to 2008, America lost 2.4 million jobs to China.[3]

For the past thirty years, China's economy has grown an average 9 to 10 percent each year. But under President Barack Obama, China has experienced unusually fast gains and America unusually fast losses. In the first quarter of 2011 alone, China's economy grew a robust 9.7 percent. America's first quarter growth rate? An embarrassing and humiliating 1.9 percent.[4] It's a national disgrace, and Barack Obama's inept policies and weak response to China's manipulation of its currency, assault on our jobs, and attack on our manufacturing base have made things worse—*far worse*—than they would otherwise have been. And yet, every time you turn on the television, what do you hear from Obama? Happy-talk rhetoric. It's like that old "prosperity is right around the corner" mantra Herbert

Hoover repeated when America was in the throes of the Great Depression. It's a lot of hot air. We've got 14.4 million of our people out of work. We need action.

America's relationship with China is at a crossroads. We only have a short window of time to make the tough decisions necessary to keep our standing in the world. Roughly every seven years, the Chinese economy doubles in size. That's a tremendous economic achievement, and it's also why they clean our clocks year in and year out on trade. Right now, we are running a massive $300 billion trade deficit with China.[5] That means every year China is making almost $300 billion off the United States. When I go on television talk shows and news programs, I say that number and people can't even wrap their minds around a figure like that, but it's true. Just on the trade imbalance alone, China is banking almost a trillion of our dollars every three years. And sadly, whereas American manufacturing used to rule the day, now, because China cheats with its currency, American companies can't compete on price, despite the fact that we make a far better product. So China is now the world's top manufacturer and exporter. By the way, they also hold more than $3 trillion of foreign reserves.[6] That's enough money for China to buy a controlling interest in every large company in the Dow Jones Industrial Average—companies like Alcoa, Caterpillar, Exxon Mobil, and Walmart—and still have billions left in the bank.[7]

One out of every six people on the planet is Chinese. Their population of 1.3 billion people outnumbers us roughly four to one. That's a huge pool of talent from which to build businesses, staff manufacturing facilities, fill elite educational institutions, and build an enormous and lethal military.

The other great concern is the fact that China graduates 7 million university students every single year. So far America still remains way ahead of China on college graduation rates as a percentage of our total population, but you have to ask whether our colleges are graduating students with the skills they need to compete. I read too many stories about corporations that have to offer remedial education classes for their employees. And when you look at test scores for middle school and high schools, there's cause for alarm. In a 2010 authoritative international study of 15-year-olds, Americans ranked twenty-fifth out of thirty-four nations in math. China's rank? Number one.[8] In fact, the Shanghai students who were studied not only were number one in math, but in reading and science as well. They just absolutely ate our lunch—and everyone else's. Sure, maybe the study was a little skewed because they sampled kids from Shanghai where many of China's smartest students go to school. But as even liberal *TIME* magazine points out, when you consider the enormous demographic changes America is undergoing, there's educational danger on the horizon. In a generation we will be a majority-minority nation, and currently a heartbreaking 40 percent of African-American and Latino-American children don't even graduate from high school (to say nothing of college).[9]

In China's Crosshairs

Where do you think Communist Chinese President Hu Jintao plans to direct most of China's educational and economic edge? That's right, the military and weapons industries. A new report from the Pentagon reveals that China is rapidly beefing up its army and navy and pouring billions of dollars into developing its first stealth fighter jet, advanced attack submarines, sophisticated air defense systems, high-tech space warfare systems, and adding to its ballistic missile stockpile.[10] In response to China's military buildup, Chairman of the Joint Chiefs of Staff Admiral Michael Mullen said this: "The Chinese have every right to develop the military they want. What I just have not been able to crack is why on some of these capabilities, whether it's [the J-20 stealth fighter], whether it's anti-satellite, whether it's anti-ship, many of these capabilities seem to be focused very specifically on the United States."[11]

What China is doing on the cyber warfare front is equally alarming. In his congressional commission testimony, Vice Chairman of the Joint Chiefs of Staff General James Cartwright said that China is heavily involved in cyber reconnaissance of American corporate and government networks. General Cartwright explained that cyber spying can isolate network weaknesses and allow the Chinese to steal valuable intelligence.[12]

So what should we do?

China presents three big threats to the United States in its outrageous currency manipulation, its systematic attempt to destroy our manufacturing base, and its industrial espionage and cyber warfare against America. The Chinese have been running roughshod over us for years. But the Obama administration, in its incredible weakness, seems almost complicit in wanting to help the Chinese trample us. Obama claims we can't do what's in our interests because it might spark a "trade war"—as if we're not in one now. And if we are in trade war, Obama's policies amount to virtual economic treason. Still, I believe we can overcome China's threats with a smart strategy and a strong negotiator.

China's massive manipulation of its currency is designed to boost its exports and wreck our domestic industries. When the Chinese government manipulates the yuan (China's currency, sometimes also called the renminbi) and undervalues it, they are able to sell to other countries at a far, far lower price than a U.S. company, because our currency is valued at a more accurate market rate. That means our products are priced higher, which makes them less competitive.

Many analysts have tried to determine the actual value of China's currency, but it's hard to say for sure, since valuations change all the time. There does, however, seem to be a consensus that the yuan is likely undervalued somewhere in the neighborhood of 40 to 50 percent of its true value.[13] That means the Chinese can charge up to half the price an American manufacturer would for a similar good or service. That spells job losses for American workers, and that's exactly what's happening right now.

Just look at what China's monetary manipulation did to our steel industry. As a builder of huge luxury buildings, I can tell you that the steel industry has been vital to our economic strength, and is an important cost in any building. According to the American Iron and Steel Institute (AISI), China's currency undervaluation represents "the single-largest subsidy" to Chinese manufacturers, is the "key" to China's explosive export-driven growth, and is "a major cause" of global structural imbalances that helped bring about America's recent financial collapse.

China's currency manipulation and other unfair trade practices helped China's crude steel production jump from 15 percent of world production in 2002 to a jaw-dropping 47 percent in 2008. In 2002, the United States imported just 600,000 tons of steel (3 percent of our steel imports) from

China. By 2008, China had us buying 5 million tons of steel.[14] And again, much of this they achieved by undervaluing the yuan.

Economist Alan Tonelson got it right when he wrote:

> For eight long years, Washington's China lobby—lavishly funded by multinational companies whose China facilities benefit from this 50 percent subsidy [from the undervalued yuan]—has trotted out rationalizations for inaction. The disastrous costs already incurred of following the China lobby's advice amply justify ignoring its latest ploy.... American factories have kept closing, survivors' profits have kept shriveling and even vanishing, job losses have kept mounting, and wages have kept sagging. Worse, U.S.-centric global economic imbalances kept mounting until they triggered the biggest American and worldwide downturn since the Great Depression.[15]

Other observers, like Republican Senator Richard Shelby of Alabama, have their eyes wide open too. "There is no question that China manipulates its currency to subsidize its exports," said Shelby. As for China buying U.S. Treasury bonds, Shelby said, "It may be time for new legislation to ensure that Treasury looks out for American workers, not Chinese creditors."[16]

As the world's leading economy, we get hurt most by China's abusive trading practices—and anyone who knows anything about economics knows I'm right. As CNN Money reported, "Most economists would agree with Trump's logic that China is holding down the value of its currency to give its manufacturers an advantage when selling goods to the U.S."[17]

Of course, back in 2008 during the presidential campaign, Barack Obama was more than happy to sound off on the negative effects of currency manipulation. As a candidate, he even endorsed a bill that would have changed the current law to "define currency manipulation as a subsidy subject to the imposition of countervailing duties."[18] Fast forward to 2011. Today, Obama is all nicey-nice on the subject and engaged in his usual "pretty please" diplomacy with the Chinese. Just listen to what the president is saying now about the Chinese undervaluing their currency to rip us off: "So we'll continue to look for the value of China's currency to be increasingly driven by the market, which will help ensure that no nation has an undue economic advantage."

That statement is drenched in weakness. "We'll continue to look" for the Chinese to magically turn from their wicked ways? Is this is a joke? As if by some miracle the Communist regime that's making $300 billion off us each year is going to wake up tomorrow and decide, "You know what, we really ought to play more fairly with the Americans and stop poaching all their jobs and companies and billions of dollars." It's ludicrous.

And by the way, shouldn't *our* president be looking out for *our* economic interests instead of protecting *other* nations' economic standing so that "no nation has an undue economic advantage"? Let's get real. China's economy is on track this year to enjoy 10.5 percent growth. The rest of the world is on pace for an average 4.8 percent growth. America? In September 2011, the U.S. GDP was an embarrassing 1.3 percent.[19] Our president should stop trying to be an economist to the world and start fighting for our economy. Instead he's putting us farther behind. He even has the audacity to *brag* about our one-sided trading relationship with China.

"We're now exporting more than $100 billion a year to China in goods and services," Obama said. "And as a result of deals we completed this week, we'll be increasing U.S. exports to China by more than $45 billion and China's investment in America by several billion dollars. Most important, these deals will support some 235,000 American jobs, and that includes a lot of manufacturing jobs."[20]

How can the president even say this with a straight face? Yes, we're exporting $100 billion in products to China, but the point is that they are exporting four times as much and banking $300 billion off us because they lie about their currency! But does he mention that? No. And notice how he says his negotiated $45 billion in exports to Communist China will "support" 235,000 American jobs. That means, we're not creating new jobs, we're just "supporting" jobs not yet destroyed by Obamanomics. So if you're lucky enough to have a manufacturing job in aviation you might get to keep it—you'll just be building planes for Hu Jintao.

The president needs to get serious with the Chinese and threaten serious sanctions if they won't play by market rules. He shouldn't be bragging about pitiful "deals" to "support" American jobs, he should be negotiating hard for real reform that would give American manufacturers a level playing field with their Chinese opponents. Then we'll see who can really clean whose clocks and create real, new private sector jobs.

Made in the U.S.A.

I'm sick of always reading about outsourcing. Why aren't we talking about "onshoring"? We need to bring manufacturing jobs back home where they belong. Onshoring, or "repatriation," is a way for us to take back the jobs China is stealing. We know that China's wages are increasing. Also, China lacks certain natural resources that we have in abundance. If we exploit those two key facts, we can begin making the case to companies that they should bring their manufacturing facilities home to America.

Some smart people are already working on this. Harry Moser, a former CEO of a U.S. manufacturing technology supplier, has started something called the Reshoring Initiative, a group that shows businesses and the government how they can make more money and build a better business through onshoring. "This trend is real," says Moser, "and it's more than a trickle, it's a steady stream." [21] Moser is right. I recently read an article in *NewsMax* magazine about a chopstick company in Americus, Georgia, called Georgia Chopsticks. The company's owners, David Hughes and Jae Lee, realized that there's tons of the special kind of wood you have to use to make chopsticks in southern Georgia. They realized they could make their chopsticks in America for cheaper than they could in China. Better still, they knew they could create more American jobs that way. So they make the chopsticks in Georgia and ship them to China! How great is that? Right now they make 4 million chopsticks a day—and they're about to up production to 10 million a day, which will create 150 new American jobs. "I'm proud to be a part of this," said Susan White, a Georgia Chopsticks employee. "It seems like everything you see in the United States these days is made in China, from clothes to even American flags. We're giving back. It's awesome." [22]

Onshoring has huge potential. But Harry Moser says the Obama administration isn't interested. "It's been a challenge getting [Obama] to embrace this. All his chips are on exporting." [23] That's why Congress needs to pass Virginia Congressman Frank Wolf's bill called the "Bring Jobs Back to America Act" (H.R. 516) to help expand the onshoring movement and get American jobs back where they belong—here in America. Look, if we can make chopsticks in America and sell them to the Chinese, we can compete on hundreds of other fronts as well. We just have to get tough, get smart, and get a president willing to stand up for America and stick it to the Chinese.

Right now we're simply getting hustled by the Chinese—and most Chinese people I deal with on a business level know it and are amazed at what Obama lets the Chinese government get away with. A tough negotiator can make the Chinese back off. We've done it before. A great example was when the Bush administration spent two years pressuring China to increase the value of the yuan relative to the dollar.[24] It worked. Between 2005 and 2008, the yuan's value rose 21 percent.[25] Since then, however, China has stopped allowing its money to appreciate, and we're in terrible shape because of it. The point is: the Chinese are smart—they respond to economic pressure, and they know they're not going to get any from Obama.

Getting China to stop playing its currency charades can begin whenever we elect a president ready to take decisive action. He could start by signing into law a bill the U.S. House of Representatives approved on a 348 to 79 vote in September 2010. It would allow our government to calculate taxes on imports based on how much the manufacturing country's currency is undervalued. Sounds like a great idea, right? But no sooner did the bill pass the House than Obama's Treasury Secretary Tim Geithner warned us that we had to be nice to China. "It's important to recognize that we're not going to have a trade war," Geithner said. "We're not going to have a currency war. I would say that a substantial fraction of the Chinese leadership understands it is very important to them economically to let this exchange rate move." Then why don't we make them do something about it, Secretary Geithner? It's the utter weakness and failure to fight for American interests from Geithner and Obama that have left us underwriting China's economic rise and our own economic collapse.

Open markets are the ideal, but if one guy is cheating the whole time, how is that free trade? Just look at the classical laws of economics, derived from that great Scotsman Adam Smith. People who know very little about capitalism summarize Adam Smith's epic book, *The Wealth of Nations*, as saying, in essence, that "greed is good," as the old line from the movie *Wall Street* put it. Like most people, I think that line is witty and made for Hollywood, but that's not what Adam Smith said in that book, nor is it what he really meant. That's why most people who bash capitalism and Adam Smith never took the time to read the book he wrote before *The Wealth of Nations*, which laid out the moral ground rules for markets, business, and life. It was a book called *The Theory of Moral Sentiments*, and it's definitely worth picking up. As Smith writes, "The man who barely abstains from violating either the person, or the estate, or the reputation of his neighbors, has surely very little positive merit."[26]

No More Currency Manipulation

It's a plain fact: free trade requires having fair rules that apply to everyone. And if we had a president who pressed the Chinese to abide by the rules, the benefits to our economy would be enormous. The Peterson

Institute for International Economics has studied the Chinese currency issue extensively and concluded that a revaluation of just 20 percent (less than half the presumed fair market rate) would create 300,000 to 700,000 American jobs over the next two to three years.[27] Think about that. Right now we have a president and a Treasury secretary who shrug while China tears away hundreds of thousands of manufacturing jobs from the United States. That's leadership? The problem is so bad and the solution so obvious that even *New York Times* columnist (and radical lefty "economist") Paul Krugman has had to concede the point: "In normal times, I'd be among the first people to reject claims that China is stealing other peoples' jobs, but right now it's the simple truth," writes Krugman. "Something must be done about China's currency." When an Obama worshipper like Paul Krugman is forced to admit there's a problem, you know America's in deep trouble.[28]

Some take the Obama approach and simply shrug at China's systematic destruction of American manufacturing. They think there's no way to revitalize that sector of our economy—and the millions of jobs that go with it. They think we can do just fine as a service-based economy. But that's just wrong. There's no reason to sacrifice millions of jobs and the future of important American industries to China just because our leaders won't get tough and defend our interests.

Here's the solution: get tough. Slap a 25 percent tax on China's products if they don't set a real market value on their currency. End of story. You think the Chinese wouldn't respond constructively? No businessman I know would want to turn his back on the U.S. market—and the Chinese wouldn't either. But it would help close the outrageous trade deficit driven by China's cheating. CNBC analyst and UC Irvine business professor Peter Navarro points out that our trade deficit is costing us roughly 1 percent of GDP growth each year, which is a loss of almost 1 million jobs annually. "That's millions of jobs we have failed to create over the last decade," writes Navarro. "And if we had those jobs now, we wouldn't see continuing high unemployment numbers, padlocked houses under foreclosure and empty factories pushing up weeds.... When a mercantilist China uses unfair trade practices to wage war on our manufacturing base, the American economy is the big loser." [29]

It's hardly any wonder that our country's manufacturing dominance has evaporated. We have a president who has a vendetta against businesspeople and considers them the enemy. He's also clueless about manufacturing. And he seems to have no regard for how China is conducting massive industrial espionage against the United States.

Stop Stealing Our Technology

American corporations and entrepreneurs are masters of technological and business innovation, but the Chinese are equally expert at stealing our trade secrets and technology. American investors and companies can pour millions of dollars into creating and developing a new product, only to have the Chinese, through industrial espionage, steal all that information for nothing. The Chinese laugh at how weak and pathetic our government is in combating intellectual property theft. That would be bad enough, but our government also stands by and does nothing while China demands that any American company that wants to enter the Chinese market has to transfer its technology to China. Such forced technology transfers are actually banned by the World Trade Organization as an unfair trade practice, but Obama lets China get away with it.[30]

Josh Kraushaar of the *National Journal* has noted that Obama's economic cluelessness has hurt him with blue collar workers. While Obama is obsessed with "green collar jobs," blue collar workers aren't buying it. "Clean-energy jobs may be the future, but they're not seen by displaced workers as a panacea."[31] The reason why blue collar workers dismiss Obama's happy-talk rhetoric is because they're smart. They know that anytime you hear this guy talk about how innovations in green technology are going to spark huge job opportunities, it's all meaningless, because Obama lacks the spine and the guts to take on China's wholesale thievery of U.S. technology and trade secrets.

And it could easily get worse, threatening not only our economy but our national security. China is a major aggressor in the field of cyber espionage and cyber warfare. It has the capacity not only to steal highly classified U.S. military technology, but to unleash crippling computer viruses on our networks. About twelve years ago, I wrote a book called *The America We Deserve*. As somebody who has written many bestsellers, including many #1 bestsellers, it was probably my least successful book. The fact is, people didn't want to hear from Donald Trump about politics but about business. That's why when I wrote *The Art of the Deal* and many of my other books, they were huge successes. In fact, *The Art of the Deal* is said to be the biggest-selling business book of all time. Nevertheless, I was proud of *The America We Deserve* for a number of reasons. First, I strongly predicted terrorism in this country, something which happened, unfortunately, and which could have been avoided or minimized. I even included

Osama bin Laden by name. Second, I predicted the crash of the economy. There were too many signs, too many signals, too many factors that I thought made the coming crash obvious. So while it was probably my least successful because it didn't discuss business, I have been given great credit for the book's powerful and accurate predictions. In this book, I'm not looking to make predictions, I'm looking to make a difference and warn about other potential threats.

I fear that a similar but different type of long-term threat exists with China's rapidly expanding military technology developments. According to the Pentagon, China's military has also made "steady progress" in developing online warfare tactics.[32]

For a country like China, being able to steal our military designs represents hundreds of billions in savings on research and development costs. After all, why spend trillions building and testing complex weapons systems when you can just poach the blueprints for free with a click of a mouse?

Just look at what's already happening right now. In 2009, the *Wall Street Journal* reported that cyber-intruders successfully copied several terabytes of highly classified data on our $300 billion Joint Strike Fighter project, which would make it far easier to defeat the new fighter, the F-35 Lightning II.[33] Not surprisingly, U.S. officials have concluded with a "high level of certainty" that the attack came from—you guessed it—China.[34]

We also now know that the People's Liberation Army (PLA) has adopted a new doctrine known as the Integrated Network Electronic Warfare (INEW). The Communist government's new plan involves "training and equipping its force to use a variety of IW [Information Warfare] tools for intelligence gathering and to establish information dominance over its adversaries during a conflict."[35] In a congressional commission, General James Cartwright testified that China is actively engaging in "cyber reconnaissance" and is penetrating the computer networks of American government agencies as well as private companies.[36] For those China apologists who might claim that these cyber attacks may have been carried out by Chinese hackers and are operating independent from the Communist government, RAND's extensive study proved exactly the opposite:

> A review of the scale, focus, and complexity of the overall campaign directed against the United States and, increasingly, a host of other countries around the world strongly suggest that these operations are state-sponsored or supported. The operators appear to have access to financial, personnel, and analytic resources that exceed what organized cybercriminal operations or multiple hacker groups operating independently could likely access consistently over several years. Furthermore, the categories of data stolen do not have inherent monetary value like credit card numbers or bank account information that is often the focus of cybercriminal organizations. Highly technical defense engineering information, military related information, or government policy analysis documents are not easily monetized by cybercriminals unless they have a nation-state customer.[37]

The military threat from China is gigantic—and it's no surprise that the Communist Chinese government lies about how big its military budget is.

The Chinese claim that it's $553 billion a year, which is about one-fifth the size of our own. But regional security experts believe that China's real military budget is much higher. One way the Chinese hide their military spending is by assigning it to other departments of government. That way their rapid military expansion can be kept secret from other nations, which, if they knew China's true military budget, might feel alarmed enough to ramp up their own spending.[38] As leaked 2009 cables revealed, Beijing's tactic of deception follows the grandfather of modern China Deng Xiaoping's admonition that China hide its capabilities while biding its time.[39]

Look, when it comes to China, America better stop messing around. China sees us as a naïve, gullible, foolish enemy. And every day Obama remains in office, they take huge strides to overtake us economically. They manipulate their currency in a way that steals a million American jobs and inflates an utterly unfair trade imbalance by $300 billion. They rip off our business's trade secrets so they can save billions in research and development costs and shave years off the time it takes to get a new product to market. And to top it all off, China is leading the way in developing advanced new cyber warfare techniques to serve as a force multiplier of their already massive military, which currently stands at 2,285,000 active troops with another 800,000 reserves. But remember one thing when we go to the negotiating table with China: Japan, a much smaller country with far fewer people and soldiers, kicked China's ass in war—not a good sign for China's warrior-like future.

We need a president who will sign the bipartisan legislation to force a proper valuation of China's currency. We need a president who will slap the Chinese with a 25 percent tax on all their products entering America if they don't stop undervaluing the yuan. We need a president who will crack down on China's massive and blatant intellectual property theft that allows China to pirate our products (maybe if Obama didn't view entrepreneurs and businesspeople as the enemy he'd be more aggressive about this). Most of all, we need a president who is smart and tough enough to recognize the national security threat China poses in the new frontier of cyber warfare.

It may seem to many that I speak very badly about China and its representatives. The truth is I have great respect for the people of China. I also have great respect for the people that represent China. What I don't respect is the way that we negotiate and deal with China. Over the years, I have done many deals and transactions with the Chinese. I have made a tremendous amount of money. I have sold apartments for $53 million, $33 million, and many at smaller numbers. I built one of the largest jobs in Manhattan with Chinese partners and made a great deal of money. So I know the Chinese, and understand and respect the Chinese.

Whenever I speak badly of what they are doing to us, I am not blaming them—I am blaming our leaders and representatives. If we could get away with it against them, I would strongly encourage us to do so. Unfortunately, they are too smart and our leaders are not smart enough.

I have many friends in China who cannot believe that their leaders are able to make such unbelievably favorable deals. I can understand it more easily than they can. Our leaders are rather, to put it succinctly, stupid. The amazing thing is, despite all of the hard rhetoric and strong words I use against China, *Bloomberg Businessweek* recently did an article about the thing the Chinese most want. Notable is a quote by real estate president

Asher Alcobi of his Chinese clients' preferences: "Anything that has the Trump name is good."[40]

So, I speak badly of China, but I speak the truth and what do the consumers in China want? They want Trump. You know what that means? That means that they respect people who tell it like it is and speak the truth, even if that truth may not be so nice towards them. In fact, it is my respect for the Chinese that leads me to tell our leaders to be careful. The Chinese will take and take and take until we have nothing left—and who can blame them if they can get away with it?

China is our enemy. It's time we start acting like it…and if we do our job correctly, China will gain a whole new respect for the United States, and we can then happily travel the highway to the future with China as our friend.

FOUR

IT'S YOUR MONEY—
YOU SHOULD KEEP
MORE OF IT

*The paradoxical truth is that the tax rates are too high today
and tax revenues are too low and the soundest way to raise
revenues in the long run is to cut rates now.*[1]

—**President John F. Kennedy**

The first sixteen hours of your forty-hour workweek you work for free. Put another way, the first four and a half months of the entire year, you work for absolutely nothing—the government confiscates every last penny of your hard-earned money in the form of taxes.

That's terrible. The economic robbery of it all is offensive enough, but equally infuriating is the amount of freedom and time the government is stealing from you as well. Imagine having sixteen hours more each week to spend with your family, or volunteering sixteen more hours every week at your favorite charity, or spending sixteen additional hours each week working on your business or next entrepreneurial venture. Imagine your paycheck was 40 percent higher than it currently is. What could you do with 40 percent more wealth? How many jobs and opportunities for others could you create? The longer you really think about it the madder you will get, especially when you consider the waste, fraud, and abuse the federal government traffics in as it inflicts its self-defeating policies on hard-working Americans.

But does that stop Obama and his "progressive" pals? No. In fact, they think the real problem isn't that your taxes are too high but that they are too *low. If only those stingy wage-earners would cough up more cash*, the administration reasons, *benevolent government bureaucrats could redistribute it more fairly and wisely.*

Look, paying taxes is a part of life, and we need to fund the things individuals can't do for themselves, like national defense and infrastructure, and yes, Social Security, Medicare, and Medicaid. "Render unto Caesar the things which are Caesar's, and unto God the things that are God's," the Gospel of Matthew reminds us. But as one fellow Christian told me, "God only asks me to tithe 10 percent to do His good works. Obama wants far, far more."

Judging from their actions, progressives don't even believe their own hype. Anyone who thinks they should pay higher taxes is free to send more money to the federal government. There's no law that says you can't pay additional taxes. In 1843 the Treasury Department established a special fund that remains to this day, called the "Gifts to the United States Government Fund" for "individuals wishing to express their patriotism to the United States."[2] Citizens can send in their checks at any time. But when the average American already spends more in taxes than they do on food, shelter, and clothing combined, it's not hard to see why very few would do such a thing. Making mountains of money and creating millions of jobs would be a far more "patriotic" gesture than fattening an already morbidly obese federal government.

In 2002, at the state level, an enterprising Virginia Delegate, Republican Kirkland Cox, set up a "Tax Me More Fund" in Virginia to see if the people who scream loudest about wanting higher taxes would put their money where their mouths were. To date, over the last eight years, the fund has netted a laughable $12,887, an amount so tiny it can't even fund the salary of a single part-time state worker.[3] Bottom line: if liberals really thought giving more of their hard-earned money to government was a great idea, they would do it. But they don't.

No doubt you work hard for your money—I know I do—and you should be permitted to keep more of it. Anything less creates a disincentive for a strong national work ethic. President Ronald Reagan, saw it the same way:

> The more government takes in taxes, the less incentive people have to work. What coal miner or assembly-line worker jumps at the offer of overtime when he knows Uncle Sam is going to take sixty percent or more of his extra pay?...Any system that penalizes success and accomplishment is wrong. Any system that discourages work, discourages productivity, discourages economic progress, is wrong.

If, on the other hand, you reduce tax rates and allow people to spend or save more of what they earn, they'll be more industrious; they'll have more incentive to work hard, and money they earn will add fuel to the great economic machine that energizes our national progress. The result: more prosperity for all—and more revenue for government.[4]

As with most things, President Reagan had it right. But Reagan wasn't the only president who understood that lower taxes yield higher revenues by unleashing economic growth and job creation. To many Democrats' chagrin, Reagan was merely echoing the economic thoughts of President John F. Kennedy, who had already said, in 1962, "The paradoxical truth is that the tax rates are too high today and tax revenues are too low and the soundest way to raise revenues in the long run is to cut rates now."[5]

Reagan and Kennedy's views prove that smart tax policy shouldn't be a partisan issue. It should be common sense. If you tax something you get less of it. It's as simple as that. The more you tax work, the less people are willing to work. The more you tax investments, the fewer investments you'll get. This isn't rocket science.

But Obama isn't interested in common sense. He's too busy using class warfare rhetoric to try to make you forget the disaster of his first term and give him a second. Take, for example, his rants and temper tantrums about making evil corporate jet owners pay higher taxes. If I thought for a minute that this was the solution to our $15 trillion debt, I would endorse it. But calling for higher taxes on private jet owners is a political joke. In fact, as the *Washington Post* points out, it's such an embarrassing idea that the

White House couldn't even come up with an estimate for the amount of revenue such a proposal would generate. Still, others estimate the amount it would take in over ten years would be $3 billion.[6] That's 0.0002 percent of the national debt. Not only would a jet tax do absolutely nothing to put a dent in the debt, it would also have a negative economic impact on the workers who manufacture and maintain those aircraft. Don't forget all of the many jobs provided by the private jet industry...including the much-needed manufacturing jobs.

That's the kind of empty, unserious rhetoric we get from this president. Obama bashes rich people and then vacations with them at Martha's Vineyard before jetting around the country doing million-dollar campaign fundraisers with rich liberals. All this from a guy who lectured Americans about tightening their belts, eating their peas, and not vacationing in Vegas to gamble at casinos. (I can't believe he can win the state of Nevada with his statements and its very high unemployment.)

Obama's Clueless on Taxes

Obama needs to wake up, stop taking so many vacations (I've never seen anything like it), and quit messing around. He also needs to learn how the real world of business operates. Everyone knows that the worst thing to do during a recession or an economic downturn is to raise taxes on anyone. It may be an inconvenient truth for the president and his horrific economic team, but business owners are the people who create jobs. Two-thirds of all jobs created in America are created by small business owners. With unemployment soaring under this president, you would think he would want to do everything he can to get unemployment down and hiring up. But he doesn't. Instead, he and his political advisors think trashing wealth creators and companies will score political points and somehow spare him defeat in 2012.

He's wrong. People are smart. They know you can't be "for" jobs but against those who create them. It doesn't work. All raising taxes on businesses does is force business owners to lay off employees they can no longer afford. It also drives up prices, encourages businessmen and women to move their businesses (and their jobs) to other countries that have far lower tax rates and regulatory costs, and sends people scrambling for tax shelters. The kid on the side of the street with a lemonade stand knows that, but not this guy. He's never worked in the private sector or made a payroll. And for a president who likes to showcase how hip and tech savvy he is, Obama also appears surprisingly clueless about how easy it is now for anyone to outsource jobs to foreign workers with just the click of a mouse. In our broadband, high-speed Internet world, the old brick-and-mortar barriers of business have vanished. That means capital can now pivot instantly to dodge ever-increasing government regulations and taxes.

Obama isn't the only one who's hazy eyed about the reality of taxes in America. In fact, lots of people have bought into the liberal lies we've heard for decades. The first of these is the one about how the middle and lower classes pay the overwhelming majority of the tax burden, letting the rich off the tax hook. If people would just stop and think about how loony this is, they would see that the very notion defies the laws of math. For starters, half of America doesn't even pay a single penny in federal income taxes.[7] That may shock you, but it's true. That's one of the reasons soaring federal spending is so dangerous: half the country shrugs its shoulders and says,

"Who cares? It's not my money they're spending." So the idea that the lower class is shouldering the tax burden is absurd, because the bottom half of Americans pay no federal income tax at all.

There's more. The top 1 percent of wage-earners in America pay for more than the entire bottom 95 percent—*combined*. And the top 10 percent of income earners foot 71 percent of the federal income tax bill.[8] "To put this in perspective," says Scott Hodge at the Tax Foundation, "the top 1 percent is comprised of just 1.4 million taxpayers and they pay a larger share of the income tax burden now than the bottom 134 million taxpayers."[9] The always business savvy Neil Cavuto from Fox News puts it this way:

> It'd be like going out to dinner with friends. Your buddy at the table picks up the bill, and some knucklehead has the audacity to say, "Joe, you should have left a bigger tip." Now, some Democrats promoting the class war say, "Good, that's the way it should be. And yeah, Joe, you should have left a bigger tip." But when you realize that the richest among us are paying for the bounty of the government for us.... We should at least, now and then, try a thank-you.[10]

I don't need a thank-you note from anyone. I make lots of money and pay lots of taxes. That's fine. But the misinformation and lies so-called "progressives" spew is ridiculous. Why demonize rich people? Who doesn't want to get rich? How do these people think charities get funded? Who do they think creates jobs? Rich people, business people, people who work very, very hard!

But here's the really fascinating part—the part liberals remain clueless about: if the federal government *really* wants to "stick it" to rich folks and confiscate more of their hard-earned money to fund their insane spending sprees on counterproductive social programs then they should *lower*, not raise, tax rates. As my friend Steve Forbes explains, before President Reagan instituted the Reagan tax cuts, the richest 1 percent of Americans paid 18 percent of all federal income taxes. The top marginal rates then went from a suffocating 70 percent down to 28 percent. And what was the result? Their portion of the national tax bill actually *doubled*—they paid 36 percent of federal income taxes and produced 23 percent of the nation's income.[11] As President Reagan explained, "A few economists call this principle supply-side economics. I just call it common sense."[12]

The reason this country is an economic disaster right now is because Barack Obama doesn't understand how wealth is created–and how the federal government can destroy it. He also doesn't understand just how mobile wealth is today. People now have options. Individuals and businesses can play ball anywhere in the world. For example, Ireland's corporate tax rate is 12.5 percent. America's? We're the second highest in the world, just behind Japan at a ridiculous 39 percent. That means businessmen can save up to 26.5 percent in taxes just by relocating their business abroad. And they are—in droves. In fact, the international average corporate tax rate is 26 percent.[13] Even socialist economies understand that high corporate taxes are a death knell for jobs and economic growth. High tax rates are literally transferring wealth and jobs abroad, which only reduces the revenues the federal government would have otherwise collected.

The other thing about high corporate tax rates is that, in the end, companies aren't the ones who foot the bill, consumers do. The Tax Foundation ran the numbers and found that in 2007, the federal corporate income tax collected $370 billion. They further concluded that the average American household pays $3,190 in corporate income taxes each year.[14] Again, Barack Obama doesn't understand what Ronald Reagan understood. Here's how President Reagan explained the corrosive influence of corporate taxes on the average American:

> Some say shift the tax burden to business and industry, but business doesn't pay taxes. Oh, don't get the wrong idea. Business is being taxed, so much so that we're being priced out of the world market. But business must pass its costs of operations—and that includes taxes—on to the customer in the price of the product. Only people pay taxes, all the taxes. Government just uses business in a kind of sneaky way to help collect the taxes. They're hidden in the price; we aren't aware of how much tax we actually pay.[15]

Reagan was right. If Americans understood just how many hidden government fees and taxes are absorbed into the prices of the goods and services they buy, they would be irate. Consider the fact that for every gallon of gas you put in your car, you pay 45.8 cents in state, local, and federal taxes. So if you fill up your tank and pump twenty gallons, you just blew $9.16 on taxes. Hidden fees affect everything, even recreational and leisure activities. For example, a fisherman pays 10 percent of the sales price on sport-fishing equipment in hidden taxes, and archers foot a federal tax on arrows of 45 cents per shaft and another 11 percent on quivers. If you book a seat on a domestic flight, you pay a 7.5 percent tax on your ticket. You'll get hit with another $3.60 tax, plus an additional $2.50 security tax for each leg of your trip. If you travel abroad, there's a $16.10 international arrival/departure tax, as well as a $4.50 fee for a "passenger-facility charge." This is why the price you're quoted for an airline ticket suddenly jumps when you pay the bill.[16]

Some people have less of a problem with so-called "sin taxes" on items government wants to discourage you from using. The federal tax on a pack of cigarettes is $1.01 a pack, on a six-pack of beer it's 33 cents. Some people say, "Well, those aren't good for you anyhow, so we should tax those things higher." Similarly, heating oil, which ensures that people up north can keep their homes warm during the winter, gets taxed by most states. The point is that all these sneaky taxes are nickeling and diming Americans to death. Worse, they mask the real costs associated with big government. If the average American was aware of just how much money government poaches from their pockets each year—an estimated 40 percent of your paycheck—there would be a tax revolt that would make the Boston Tea Party look like amateur hour.[17]

It's unfair and wrong. It's also bad economic policy. When taxes go up, what do people do? Many smart people shift their money into tax-free municipal bonds. And guess what? The government doesn't get the money it thinks it's going to get. If Obama knew more about economics he'd know about something called Hauser's Law, named after W. Kurt Hauser, a chairman emeritus at the Hoover Institution at Stanford University. As Hauser explains, the top marginal personal tax rate for the last sixty years has swung wildly, ranging from as high as 92 percent in 1952–1953 all the way down to 28 percent in 1988–1990. Yet regardless of the tax rate, tax revenues as a percentage of GDP have stayed roughly the same, averaging just under 19 percent.[18] That's because when taxes get too painful, people simply move their money away from the federal government's greedy hands and into tax-free havens. High tax rates don't increase government revenues, all they do is take money out of the productive economy that creates jobs and lock it into less dynamic investments like bonds. Only a fool would advocate such a disastrous plan. But that's precisely the path Barack Obama has pursued.

None of this should have come as a surprise to anyone who was paying attention in 2008. Remember Joe the Plumber? Then-candidate Barack Obama made his intentions crystal clear: "I believe that when you spread the wealth around, it's good for everybody." So we knew where this was heading all along, because it's not government's job to spread your money around. You spread it around yourself when you decide how you want to spend it, invest it, or donate it. Obama supports taxes because he believes government should decide more and you should decide less.

Based on their words and policies, Michelle and Barack Obama apparently believe that capitalism and entrepreneurship are bad. The way they see it, raising taxes is a way to punish people for having the audacity to work hard and get rich. As First Lady Michelle Obama put it in a speech in Ohio to a women's group: "Don't go into corporate America. You know, become teachers. Work for the community. Be social workers. Be a nurse...."

Make that choice, as we did, to move out of the money-making industry into the helping industry."[19] Teachers and nurses are great, but to tell people that being in business is somehow illegitimate and not part of the "helping industry" is a horrible message to send to people. Especially young people interested in business and entrepreneurship. By her logic (if you can call it that), creating a company that creates tens of thousands of jobs and provides employees an honest way to feed their families and send their kids to college is somehow to engage in activity that is not part of the "helping industry." But again, the Obamas telegraphed their anti-wealth message all along. As President Obama confessed, "I do think at a certain point you've made enough money," as if it's his or the government's place to decide how hard you work and how much wealth and opportunity you create. It's shameful and sad. It's no wonder he's turned America into a huge train wreck.

Time to Get Smart on Taxes

We need a tax system that is fair and smart—one that encourages growth, savings, and investment. It's time to stop punishing hard work and entrepreneurship. Specifically, we need to do five things. First, the death tax needs to die. It's immoral for the government to tax you after you're dead, to seize a portion of your money and property that you spent your life building up, and on which you already paid taxes. Your children deserve your estate, not the federal government. President George W. Bush eliminated the death tax (sometimes called the estate tax) for one year. But after 2010, under Obama, it rose from the grave. Now estates, above an exempted level, will be taxed at a rate up to 35 percent. "It doesn't seem to matter that the vast majority of the money in an estate was already taxed when the money was earned," reports the *Wall Street Journal*. "This ignores that much of the long-term saving and small business investment in America is motivated by the ability to pass on wealth to the next generation.... What all this means is that the higher the estate tax, the lower the incentive to reinvest in family businesses."[20]

A study by former Congressional Budget Office director Douglas Holtz-Eakin found that moving the death tax from 0 percent to 45 percent (the amount Obama wants) is a proven jobs killer, because it will strip $1.6 trillion of small business capital out of the hands of job creators. That, says Holtz-Eakin, means a loss of 1.5 million new jobs. How can we sit back and let that happen at a time when 25 million Americans can't find enough work to take care of their families?[21] The death tax only raises a tiny 1 percent of all federal revenue.[22] Plus, heirs already have to pay capital gains on the assets they acquire from any estate. This president is willing to sacrifice 1.5 million jobs just for the pleasure of "sticking it to rich people." That's simply wrong.

Obama says that "when we think about tax reform we should be thinking about fairness. What's fair?"[23] Well, I'll tell you what's *not* fair, Mr. President: killing 1.5 million jobs and strangling economic growth just so you can feel warm and fuzzy about taking money from family businesses and spreading it around as you and your bureaucrats see fit. If we repeal the death tax, we get 1.5 million jobs, boost small business capital by more than $1.6 trillion, increase payrolls by 2.6 percent, improve the probability of businesses hiring new employees by 8.6 percent, and expand investment by 3 percent.[24] It's a no-brainer. It's time to kill the death tax once and for all. More than a million jobs depend on it.

Second, we need to lower tax rates on capital gains and dividends—two more taxes that are proven jobs and investment killers. Naturally, President Obama wants to do the opposite. He wants to raise the capital gains tax rate from 15 percent to 20 percent.[25] He also wants to jack up the dividend tax rate by the same amount. Again, in Obama's world, it's all about punishing success and redistributing wealth. As economist J. D. Foster pointed out, "Obama was very clear in his campaign debate with then-Senator Clinton that raising revenues was not his primary reason for suggesting the capital gains tax hike." Even the president's own budget numbers show that a miniscule 0.01 percentage point drop in annual economic growth—which is inevitable if Obama's tax policies are followed—would totally wipe out the money he hopes to cream off with his capital gains tax increase. J. D. Foster concludes, "The President should set aside his ideological preferences and press Congress to maintain the current 15 percent tax rates for capital gains and dividend tax rates until the economy reaches full employment." [26] To raise these tax rates now (or ever) is shortsighted and economically foolish.

Capitalism requires capital. When government robs capital from investors, it takes away the money that creates jobs—real private sector jobs that contribute to the health of our economy. For a guy who claims that creating jobs is the first thing he thinks about when he wakes up and the last thing he thinks about before he goes to sleep, you would think he would know better. But he doesn't. That's why we need a new president, one who will keep capital gains rates low.

The third thing we need to do is lower the U.S. corporate tax rate from 39 percent to zero. As I stated, America's corporate tax rate is the second highest on the planet. The international average is 26 percent. How can we expect companies to hire American workers and locate their businesses in America when our government taxes them at exorbitant rates for doing so? That's crazy. I want to encourage American companies to stay here and hire American workers, and I want foreign companies to relocate their businesses to the United States and create jobs *here*. We are the greatest country on planet earth—the world's companies want to be here. A zero percent corporate tax would create an unprecedented jobs boom. Millions of jobs would materialize. This isn't brain surgery. You cut the corporate tax and companies stay in America or relocate to America, and that produces jobs. Who doesn't understand that?

The problem is that we have a president who is more concerned with pursuing some sort of bizarre ideological mission that flies in the face of America's free-market tradition. Look, we don't have time to play games. Our people are hurting badly. Here's my message to Obama: America is a capitalist country. Get over it and get on with it! Unleash job creators and we will put Americans back to work in big numbers. Cut the corporate tax and create millions of new jobs while stimulating our limping economy.

Fourth, it's time to get tough on those who outsource jobs overseas and reward companies who stay loyal to America. If an American company outsources its work, they get hit with a 20 percent tax. For those companies who made the mistake of sending their businesses overseas but have seen the light and are ready to come home and bring jobs with them, they pay zero tax. Bottom line: hire American workers and you win. Send jobs overseas, and you may be fine, but you will pay a tax. Also, I want foreign countries to finally start forking over cash in order to have access to our markets. So here's the deal: any foreign country shipping goods into the United States pays a 20 percent tax. If they want a piece of the American market, they're going to pay for it. No more free admission into the biggest show in town—and that especially includes China.

The fifth and final part of my tax plan involves reforming the income tax. The government confiscates way too much of your paycheck. The tax code is also a very, very complicated system that forces Americans to waste 6.1 billion hours a year trying to figure it out.[27] Americans also waste billions hiring accountants to try and make sense out of the tax code. You can hire 100 accountants to do your taxes and they'll all come up with different numbers. What does that tell you? It tells me that it's time we restore simplicity and sanity to the income tax. Here's my income tax plan:

- Up to $30,000, you pay 1 percent
- From $30,000 to $100,000, you pay 5 percent
- From $100,000 to $1 million, you pay 10 percent
- On $1 million or above, you pay 15 percent

It's clear and fair. Best of all, it can be filled out on the back of a postcard and will save Americans big bucks on accountants and massive amounts of time wasted attempting to decipher the tax code.

Our country is hungry for real tax reform. That's why we should implement the 1-5-10-15 income tax plan. Let China, OPEC, and others pay the tax, not us. It's about time…and they have all the money.

❧

I believe the government already takes enough of your hard-earned money. Obama thinks the opposite. If we want jobs in America, we need to enact my five-part tax policy: kill the death tax, lower the tax rates on capital gains and dividends, eliminate corporate taxes in order to create more American jobs, mandate a 15 percent tax for outsourcing jobs and a 20 percent tax for importing goods, and enact the 1-5-10-15 income tax plan.

Government needs to stop pick-pocketing your wallet. Every time it does, it slows growth and kills jobs. It's also immoral. We need to get back to doing what we know works. President Reagan had it right: lower taxes produce more freedom and opportunity for all. Everyone knows that—except in Washington. It's time we send the politicians a big message loud and clear. As Senator Everett Dirksen once said, "When they feel the heat they'll see the light." It's time we turn up the heat.

FIVE

A GOVERNMENT WE CAN AFFORD

*A government big enough to give you everything
you want is a government big enough
to take from you everything you have.*[1]

—President Gerald Ford

Every day, your government takes in $6 billion in revenue and spends $10 billion. That means every day the federal government has to borrow $4 billion more than it has.[2]

To state the obvious, if any business operated the way the government does, it would go under. But in the absurd world of Washington, politicians just kick the can down the road and shrug. There's just one problem: the can has finally hit a $15 trillion debt wall. For the first time since the founding of the Republic, we've lost our AAA credit rating, and now even our enemy China is having second thoughts about lending us money to bankroll Barack Obama's endless spending spree.

Americans understand that the U.S. has a spending problem, not a revenue problem. In September 2011, Gallup asked Americans how much money they think the federal government wastes. On average, citizens put the figure at 51 cents out of every dollar. That's probably being too kind.

We need more grown-ups in Washington, people who will shoot straight and level with the American people about our nation's top budget busters. The biggest slices of the budgetary pie are eaten up by Social Security, Medicare, and Medicaid. Social Security makes up 20 percent of the budget ($707 billion). Medicare and Federal Medicaid account for 22 percent of the budget ($724 billion). As everyone knows, health-care costs are skyrocketing, and Medicaid has massively expanded its role in the health-care system. When Medicaid was created in 1965, only one in fifty citizens used the program. Today, it's one in six Americans.

Save Social Security and Medicaid

Social Security faces a similar problem. Soon there will be more people inside the cart than there are pulling the cart. Right now, 53 million people collect Social Security benefits that average $1,067 a month. In seventy-five years, that number will jump to 122 million, roughly one out of every four citizens.[3] That's why, with 77 million baby boomers set to retire and begin collecting benefits, these two programs—a combined 42 percent of the U.S. budget—are in danger of becoming insolvent. We can't let that happen.

Now I know there are some Republicans who would be just fine with allowing these programs to wither and die on the vine. The way they see it, Social Security and Medicare are wasteful "entitlement programs."

But people who think this way need to rethink their position. It's not unreasonable for people who paid into a system for decades to expect to get their money's worth—that's not an "entitlement," that's honoring a deal. We as a society must also make an ironclad commitment to providing a safety net for those who can't make one for themselves. At least that was President Reagan's stance. On April 20, 1983, Reagan signed a bill to preserve Social Security. At that bill signing, the president said words every Republican should heed:

> This bill demonstrates for all time our nation's ironclad commitment to Social Security. It assures the elderly that America will always keep the promises made in troubled times a half a century ago. It assures those who are still working that they, too, have a pact with the future. From this day forward, they have one pledge that they will get their fair share of benefits when they retire.[4]

President Reagan had it right: Social Security is here to stay. To be sure, we must reform it, root out the fraud, make it more efficient, and ensure that the program is solvent beyond the Baby Boomers. But to listen to some Republicans vilify a system that's been around for over seventy-six years and that taxpayers have paid into for decades makes me think they should go back and watch President Reagan's speech again.

Same goes for Medicare. Again, people have lived up to their end of the bargain and paid into the program in good faith. Of course they believe they're "entitled" to receive the benefits they paid for—they are!

The question is, how do we pay for Medicare, Medicaid, and Social Security when costs are ballooning and deficits are soaring? Here again, both sides fumble the ball badly. Democrats pretend that the answer is raising taxes. But anyone with a brain knows all that will do is kill economic growth. That's the exact opposite of what needs to happen. Economic growth is the secret to making the entire pie grow larger. When that happens, millions of new workers will become new taxpayers and revenues will rise. As Senator Marco Rubio of Florida put it: "Let's stop talking about new taxes and start talking about creating new taxpayers, which basically means jobs."[5] And that's what economic growth will do.

But many Republicans also miss the mark. They pretend we can just nibble around the edges by eliminating waste, fraud, and abuse and somehow magically make these programs solvent *and* pay off our massive $15 trillion debt. Neither side is being totally honest.

Our country doesn't need cowardice, it needs courage. Here's the first part of the solution: our leaders need to get tough with the big players like China and OPEC that are ripping us off so we can recapture hundreds of billions of dollars to pay our bills, take care of our people, and get us on a path toward serious debt reduction. We must take care of our own people—we must make our country strong and rich again so that Social Security, Medicare, and Medicaid will no longer be thought of as a problem. We must save these programs through strength, power, and wealth.

As I explained earlier, China takes us for $300 billion a *year*, and OPEC is even worse. Washington is so busy squabbling over peanuts that they're completely missing the mountains of money staring them in the face. Obama and Republicans spent weeks bickering over $60 billion of spending cuts in the president's budget. Excuse me, but we have a $15 *trillion* debt. We need to get serious and get tough with the big rip-off artists who abuse this country regularly. If we do that first, the remaining cuts and reforms we need to make will be substantially smaller, more manageable, and much less painful.

Stop and think about it: even just leveling the playing field with China for a decade would be the equivalent of one-fifth of our national debt (and would have been one-third of our debt had we not elected the community organizer). You add in several hundred billion a year from putting OPEC in line, hundreds of billions from negotiating properly with the many other countries that are ripping us off, root out the hundreds of billions of incredible fraud that occur every year (more on that later), and now we have a debt problem America can manage—one where we can attack waste and abuse and whittle down the remaining debt to get our fiscal house in order. So that's the first step: bringing home the hundreds of billions of dollars that the petro thugs at OPEC and our enemy China steal from us every single year—and then go after all of the others.

Next, we need a president who realizes that your money belongs to *you*, not him. A real president should take pride in saving and spending your money wisely, not funneling it to his cronies and political backers in the form of so-called "stimulus." But unfortunately, that's not the kind of president we currently have in the Oval Office. This guy wouldn't save the American taxpayer $100 million if it landed on his front doorstep. I should know. I tried to make a $100 million gift to the United States government, but Barack Obama wouldn't even return my phone call.

My $100 Million Gift to the U.S. Goes Uncollected

If you want a small example of just how uninterested your government is in saving and spending your money wisely, read on. One day I was watching television and I saw that President Obama was hosting a dinner for various leaders at the White House. But every time they had one of these events, I noticed that they put up an old, broken, rotten-looking tent out on the White House grounds that they probably paid some local guy a fortune for every time they needed it. That's no way for America to host important meetings and dinners with world leaders and dignitaries. We should project our nation's power and beauty with a proper facility and ballroom. If there's one thing I know how to build, it's a grand ballroom. At my private Mar-a-Lago Club in Palm Beach, Florida, I built what many consider to be the single greatest ballroom in the world... but I own many beautiful and very successful ballrooms.

So I called up the White House and they put me on with President Obama's top senior strategist, David Axelrod. We had a very nice conversation, and I told David that "I will build you, free of charge, one of the great ballrooms of the world so that the president and all future American presidents can host events at the White House in a proper manner. To do it to the highest standards, it will cost anywhere from $50 to $100 million. I will cover the expenses and give the ballroom to the U.S. government as a gift. What I will do is I will hire the top ten vying architects in the world— I hope they'll be American architects, but I'll hire the best, whoever they are. We'll then have a review committee set up. We'll pick the architect that everybody agrees on, because it's a little delicate in that it's the White House we're talking about. And I will build the greatest ballroom there is, even better than the Mar-a-Lago ballroom, so that Americans can be proud when our presidents host world leaders on the White House grounds."

"Wow," Axelrod said. "That's very interesting." He then said he would talk it over and get back to me. No one ever called back. And that's what's wrong with this country. When Rush Limbaugh invited me to come on his show I told him that story, and Rush said that they probably didn't get back to me because I'm a lifelong Republican. Rush is probably right, but I'm sure it is just the way business is done in Washington, billions of dollars are squandered and people just don't care. I really thought David would take me up on my offer but it is not too late. My offer still stands. If someone wants to give America—a nation that is flat broke—a nice gift, you call them back, regardless of what party they belong to. It's just one small example of how the Obama administration isn't fiscally wise and certainly doesn't care about taking advantage of ways to give Americans the most for less. To the Obama administration, saving money isn't the point—expanding government and spending *more* taxpayers' dollars is. Sometimes they call it "investment" or "stimulus," but a lot of it is sheer unadulterated waste.

We need a dealmaker in the White House, who knows how to think innovatively and make smart deals.

As an example, in a fairly recent well-documented Florida deal, I purchased a house in Palm Beach at a bankruptcy sale (sadly, a very rich man lost everything) for $41 million and everybody thought I was crazy. But I knew better. It was a great parcel of land fronting the ocean—and a short time later I sold it to a Russian for approximately $100 million. Had I listened to all the geniuses I wouldn't have made that deal. It's all about seeing the unseen. This is the kind of thinking we need to turn this country around—and fast.

We also need someone who can save money through common sense. When I opened Trump National Golf Club at Rancho Palos Verdes in Los Angeles, I was immediately told that I would need to build a new and costly ballroom. The current ballroom was gorgeous, but it only sat 200 people and we were losing business because people needed a larger space for their events. Building a new ballroom would take years to get approval and permits (since it's on the Pacific Ocean), and cost about $5 million. I took one look at the ballroom and saw immediately what needed to be done. The problem wasn't the size of the room, it was the size of the chairs. They were huge, heavy, and unwieldy. We didn't need a bigger ballroom, we needed smaller chairs! So I had them replaced with high-end, smaller chairs. I then had our people sell the old chairs and got more money for them than the cost of the new chairs. In the end, the ballroom went from seating 200 people to seating 320 people. Our visitors got the space they desired, and I spared everyone the hassle of years of construction and $5 million of expense. It's amazing what you can accomplish with a little common sense.

Washington Wastes Your Money

To have a government we can afford we need to eliminate the tremendous waste clogging the system. Almost every week a new story comes out reporting another gross example of government waste. The GAO reports that every year the federal government spends billions of dollars on dozens of wasteful overlapping programs. One simple fix—streamlining and consolidating 2,100 data centers—would save $200 billion over the next decade.[6]

Another example of federal government incompetence with your money: over the last five years, the Office of Personnel Management sent out $601 million in retirement benefits to people who are dead![7] The list of insane federal expenditures is almost endless: in 2010, $700,000 of your tax dollars went to research cow burps, $600,000 was spent on creating a wolf video game, and $250,000 was spent to research Internet romance.[8] And of course who can forget the $1,442,515 that the National Institutes of Health has allocated to be spent from 2008 to 2012 to study male prostitutes in Vietnam.[9] On and on it goes. Your hard-earned money blown on ridiculous junk as far as the eye can see.

Obama doesn't respect the fact that the money he wastes belongs to us. He thinks that the wealth you create belongs to the government. That's why he doesn't care whether it gets wasted or mismanaged. I, on the other hand, think wasting money is offensive and foolish. That's why I make lots of money—I manage projects tightly and put a premium on efficiency.

Case in point: the Wollman Ice Skating Rink in Central Park. My apartment in Trump Tower overlooks the skating rink, which is more than an acre in size, making it the largest man-made ice skating rink in the United States. For seven straight years, the rink was closed on account of New York City's management fiasco. The city of New York wasted seven years and $21 million and was still unable to get the rink open—it was a political nightmare and a great embarrassment to the city.

Essentially, all this bureaucracy and wasting of taxpayers' money really got to me, so I asked to take over the project and even put up the construction money myself. Furthermore, I said that if the project went over budget, I would personally pick up the overruns. I told the city I would have Wollman Rink finished in six months. I was wrong. I did it in four. And I only spent $1.8 million—and a big portion of that was demolishing all of the incompetent work that was done before I took over. Am I an expert in building ice skating rinks? No, I build luxury towers, hotels, clubs, etc. But I've never forgotten what my father used to tell me. He said, "Know everything you can about what you're doing." So I went out and found the best ice skating rink builder in America and then managed the details to a successful completion. To this day, it remains a case study in many of the leading business schools on private versus government projects. Better still, Wollman Rink provides thousands of children, families, and visitors to our great city a wonderful experience that brings lots of smiles and great memories. That's what can happen when you actually work to save, not waste, money.

Crack Down on Massive Fraud

Beyond eliminating the wasteful spending, we need to get tough in cracking down on the hundreds of billions of dollars we lose from the massive fraud committed in government programs every year. The FBI estimates that Medicare fraud alone costs you the taxpayer between $70 billion and $234 billion every single year![10] Typically, this fraud involves fake billing scams. For example, in September 2011, officials uncovered a Medicare fraud ring involving 91 individuals charged with filing $295 million in phony billings.[11] In 2010, Medicare paid out more than $35 million to 118 "phantom" medical clinics that were allegedly created by criminal gangs as part of a reimbursement racket. As *60 Minutes* revealed, South Florida has become "ground zero" for Medicare fraud because so many elderly people live there. It's become so bad down there that law enforcement says Medicare crimes have now replaced cocaine as the number one criminal enterprise in South Florida.[12]

Now stop and do the math. If the FBI's top estimates are correct, that's $2,340,000,000 in Medicare fraud over a decade—or 16 percent of America's entire national debt! And by the way, we haven't even started with Obamacare yet—a trillion dollar government boondoggle sure to unleash unbelievable corruption and criminality on the American taxpayer.

Then there's the disability racket. Did you know that one out of every twenty people in America now claims disability? That adds up to $170 billion a year in disability checks. Between 2005 and 2009, it is estimated that $25 billion were eaten up in fraudulent Social Security Disability Insurance filings.[13] Then there's the $116 million in fraud from the Low-Income Home Energy Assistance Program.[14] And the $112 million the Internal Revenue Service doled out in tax refunds to prisoners who filed fraudulent tax returns. On and on, scam after scam it goes...as always, taxpayers are the ones getting stiffed.

Negotiate Smarter

A lot of Republicans I know look at all this waste, fraud, and abuse and wonder why the GOP hasn't been better at reforming the system and getting America's fiscal house in order. Well, the sad truth is some Republicans in Congress are clueless when it comes to negotiation. Now I know this will ruffle some of my fellow conservatives' feathers, but I'm going to say it anyway. I'm sure Congressman Paul Ryan is a nice guy, but I can tell you this much: he is one lousy poker player. In an effort to talk about how he would balance the budget and rein in Washington's spending addiction, he came out with his plan to overhaul Medicare. It was an absolutely unbelievable blunder...I'm talking about his total lack of negotiating skills.

Congressman Ryan and the Republicans committed two fatal errors. First, anyone who knows anything about negotiation knows that you always make the other guy go first. Republicans should have waited the president out and forced him to go first in naming where cuts would come from and how he planned to get the budget under control and protect America's credit rating. But he didn't. Instead, Congressman Ryan committed a major mistake. He went out and put a huge target on Republicans while Obama sat back and let the GOP commit political suicide. The second mistake Ryan made was that he scared the heck out of seniors. Like it or not, the majority of seniors love Medicare. And I like it for them. When you start talking in ways that make older Americans nervous, it's bad politics.

So what did the Democrats do? They turned Paul Ryan and his Medicare proposal into a punching bag, and Republicans lost a special congressional election in upstate New York that they should have won handily. The Democratic candidate, Kathy Hochul, bludgeoned her Republican opponent Jane Corwin with a Mediscare campaign of TV ads that featured an old lady in a wheelchair being shoved off a cliff. The ad explained that the reason grandma was being tossed over the ledge was because of "Paul Ryan and his friends in Congress." Unfair? You bet. Good politics? Absolutely. The GOP needs to learn how to get tough and out-negotiate Obama and his big spending allies in Washington. They also need to learn the art of using the right tone and language.

That's certainly the case when it comes to the debate surrounding how best to fix and save Social Security. Conservatives have to be smart in the way we speak. Using crazy language that terrifies seniors accomplishes nothing. It simply hands Democrats another weapon with which to demonize Republicans as heartless and stingy. Again, when someone has worked for forty years and seen the government deduct 6 percent out of each of the 480 paychecks they received over those years, it's perfectly understandable that they would want the money they are owed. It's only fair.

So the first thing we need to remind seniors is that their Social Security is safe, secure, and will not be touched in any way whatsoever. Period. We have the funds to pay them the money they are due, and we will. Then, we need to look at the next seventy-five years and address the projected $5.3 trillion shortfall. The Democrats' solution is the same solution they have for everything—tax, tax, tax. Just one problem: it doesn't work! All that ends up happening is the government big spenders raid the Social Security trust funds and blow the dough on junk programs we don't need. Bottom line: raising taxes to shore up the funding gap isn't the way to give America a government it can afford, but making the economy strong again is.

The Solution

So what should we do? The first thing we need to realize is that, thanks to advancements in medicine and health, Americans live and work longer than in the days when Social Security began. In fact, since Social Security was created in 1935, Americans' life expectancy has increased to seventy-eight, up 26 percent, whereas the retirement age to receive full benefits has only gone up only 3 percent, to sixty-seven.[15] Today people work well into their seventies, which is absolutely wonderful. So if we slowly increased the full retirement age to even just seventy, one-third of the $5.3 trillion short-fall would be eliminated right away. And don't do it now, do it in the future.[16]

The fastest way we can start saving Social Security is to get Americans back to work. More citizens earning a paycheck means more workers paying into the system. It also means that we will save on the explosion of unemployment benefits we've seen under Barack Obama. For example, extended unemployment benefits in just the next two years will cost American taxpayers $34 billion.[17] If the goal is getting our deficits and debt under control, the quickest road to get there is to spark economic growth and let job creators do what they do best—create jobs.

The final part of restoring fiscal sanity to America is the most obvious, and that's to control Obama-style runaway spending. It's hard for most folks to wrap their minds around just how out-of-step and radical this president truly is when it comes to spending. Here's how the *Wall Street Journal* tried to paint the picture:

As for the deficit, CBO [the Congressional Budget Office] shows that over the first three years of the Obama Presidency, 2009-2011, the federal government will borrow an estimated

$3.7 trillion. That is more than the entire accumulated national debt for the first 225 years of U.S. history. By 2019, the interest payments on this debt will be larger than the budget for education, roads and all other nondefense discretionary spending.[18]

The economic idiocy of this presidency has been truly astounding. And that's why America desperately needs a president who understands and appreciates the businesses and entrepreneurs that create opportunity and jobs. But Obama spits in the face of job creators every chance he gets. Just look at the absurd tactics the Obama administration unleashed on Gibson Guitars. They raided the guitar company factories to see if they were using certain types of wood that Obama doesn't want them to use. Is this seriously how we want America to operate? Allowing the federal government to treat businesses like drug dealers because someone may have filled an order improperly is ridiculous. It's also a terrible misuse of limited resources. The fact that it only took three years for this guy to blow a hole in the national debt that's equivalent to the debt accrued in 225 years of American history shows just how radical and outside the mainstream Barack Obama is.

That said, let me be clear: I was very, very critical of President George W. Bush. I thought he betrayed his principles of fiscal conservatism by spending excessively. Furthermore, I thought that his mismanagement of Hurricane Katrina was horrible, and I questioned his judgment in launching the war in Iraq that cost us trillions in dollars and, worse, thousands in lives. But President Bush's spending excesses were nothing compared to

Obama's. In just three years, Obama has exploded our debt so that we have to borrow $4 billion every day. By comparison, under President George W. Bush, over all eight years in office, that figure was $1.6 billion a day.[19] Not great, but a lot better.

Of course, anyone who was paying attention in 2008 should have known that Obama wasn't interested in debt and deficit reduction. But the fact that he completely ignored his own debt commission's findings in the Bowles-Simpson Report proves that this president has no shame and has no intention of slowing down his spending spree. Every American, regardless of party, needs to think long and hard about what another four years of Barack Obama would mean to the national debt and the solvency of Social Security, Medicare, and Medicaid. If he had no shame in adding more to the national debt in three years than almost all other United States presidents combined, can you imagine the kind of damage he would do if given another four years without the worry of reelection? It's a horrifying thought for anyone who loves our country and wants to see her survive and thrive again.

⇒⋆⇐

Look, here's the deal: Barack Obama has been a total disaster. He has spent this country into the ground and destroyed jobs and economic growth. If something isn't done soon, programs Americans depend on, like Medicare, Medicaid, and Social Security, are going to go up in flames. It doesn't have to be this way. We can return America to her former greatness if we get tough and act smart.

It starts with China and OPEC. The hundreds of billions of dollars they steal from us each year must end right away. We need a president with a titanium spine who will stand up to these shakedown artists and demand that they get their greedy hands out of our pockets effective immediately. That one action alone will result in a windfall of hundreds of billions of dollars to help us pay down our debt and meet our commitments. Next, we enforce a zero-tolerance policy for the kind of brainless government waste that we've all become far too accustomed to from Washington. That means we streamline our systems and end the waste. Third, we go after the criminals and con artists who are defrauding taxpayers of $243 billion every year in Medicare fraud and billions more in other kinds of fraud, such as the disability racket. Sitting back while these crooks steal from hard-working people and rob deserving Americans of the benefits they paid for is vile. We must prosecute these thugs to the fullest extent of the law and recoup the hundreds of billions they take from us year in and year out. Fourth, we must save Social Security through economic success. Fifth, we need to put Americans back to work and kick the community organizer out of office so we can instill some fiscal sanity in Washington.

We do those five things and we will pass along to our kids and grandkids not only a government they can afford, but also one they can be proud of.

SIX

STRENGTHEN AMERICAN MUSCLE

*There is a rank due to the United States among nations
which will be withheld, if not absolutely lost, by the reputation
of weakness. If we desire to avoid insult, we must be able
to repel it; if we desire to secure peace, one of the
most powerful instruments of our rising prosperity,
it must be known that we are at all times ready for war.*[1]

—President George Washington

Your civil liberties mean nothing if you're dead. That's why the single most important function of the federal government is national defense.

Our Founding Fathers got it. They understood that nothing good in life—religious freedom, economic freedom, freedom of speech—can be enjoyed if people fear for their physical safety. But unfortunately, we live in a dangerous world that's getting more dangerous by the day. China is in the midst of a massive military buildup and the creation of cyber-warfare weapons capable of bringing America to its knees. Russia is rising.

Iran, which funds terrorists all over the world, is inching closer to the creation of an operational nuclear weapon. Pakistan has been exposed as the nation that harbored Osama bin Laden next to its equivalent of West Point, and its intelligence agency is assisting the Haqqani Network, a terrorist group more dangerous than al Qaeda. Afghanistan is still a mess and a terrorist hotbed. Syria is on the verge of civil war, and Libya is already engaged in one. And of course, there are always the certifiably insane dictators of Venezuela, Cuba, and North Korea.

In short, national security threats are everywhere and growing. That's why I have so much admiration and respect for the 2.4 million men and women of our Armed Forces. Every single day, our soldiers, sailors, airmen, and Marines wake up, put on a uniform, and honor their solemn pledge to defend America against our enemies. They know their lives are on the line, but they love America so much they're willing to die for her. That's a level of commitment most civilians will never experience—most of us don't have jobs that require a willingness to die for our fellow citizens. In fact, I believe we owe our veterans more than we could ever repay them. That's why I was honored to play a major role in the New York Vietnam Veterans Memorial Commission to honor our warriors with a proper memorial and help them land jobs. I put up over a million dollars to see to it that the effort was a success. I was so moved and proud to be associated with the project, because our heroes deserve the very best.

America deserves a commander in chief who respects the challenges and realities our Armed Forces face in our dangerous world. Specifically, our military deserves the best equipment, the best training, and the best weapons. They also deserve to be paid well for the dangerous and heroic work they do. They more than earn it.

If history teaches us anything, it's that strong nations require strong leaders with clearly defined national security principles. Realities change at warp speed; international events can turn on a dime. The 9-11 terrorist attacks, the wars in Iraq, Afghanistan, Libya, the Arab Spring—all these happened in the blink of an eye. A president can't always predict where the next national security "fire" will erupt, but he can and must have a steady and reliable compass to guide his decisions. Citizens need to know the values and principles their president will rely on to lead America through whatever unknown threats lie over the horizon. I believe that any credible American foreign policy doctrine should be defined by at least seven core principles:

1. American interests come first. Always. No apologies.
2. Maximum firepower and military preparedness.
3. Only go to war to win.
4. Stay loyal to your friends and suspicious of your enemies.
5. Keep the technological sword razor sharp.
6. See the unseen. Prepare for threats before they materialize.
7. Respect and support our present and past warriors.

Sadly, President Obama has undermined each of these core principles. First, no sooner had he been sworn into office than he went on an apology tour to the Arab world. Did you know that the very first interview Obama gave as president was with the Arabic news channel Al Arabiya?[2] I've got news for President Obama: America is *not* what's wrong with the world. I don't believe we need to apologize for being hated by Islamic radical terrorists who hate our religion, hate our freedom, and hate that we extend human rights to women. Second, even as Obama's blown trillions of our tax dollars on his "stimulus" schemes, he's proposed cutting $400 billion from our defense budget. Third, by announcing the time and date for withdrawal in Afghanistan and not clearly defining our objectives in Libya's civil war, Obama has completely blown it, making it virtually impossible for us to define what victory is and achieve it. Fourth, the president sold out our dear friend and ally Israel. He's also thrown other allies, like Poland and the Czech Republic, under the bus by bowing to Russian demands that we not build missile defenses to protect our friends. Fifth, by slashing military budgets Obama has threatened our ability to keep our technological edge in weapons systems. Sixth, Obama has been caught flatfooted by China's development of the J-20 fighter jet, something his administration didn't think would happen for years to come. And finally, by raiding the defense budget to pay for his failed social programs, Obama continues to weaken our ability to honor our present and past warriors.

When our military and intelligence officers located Osama bin Laden, right smack in the middle of Pakistan, they went to the president to inform him and asked whether or not he should be taken out by a missile or in a raid (either solution being okay). The only other option would have been to let him be. Well, Obama had a decision a make. We have bin Laden—do we leave him alone? I can't believe that anybody sitting in the Oval Office would have said, "Let's do nothing." So he really had only one choice to

My father lived the American dream. The son of German immigrants, he became an entrepreneur and created jobs and wealth and homes for thousands of people. My wonderful mother was an immigrant from Scotland.

Here I am, on the end, with my brothers Fred Jr. and Robert, and my sisters Maryanne and Elizabeth.

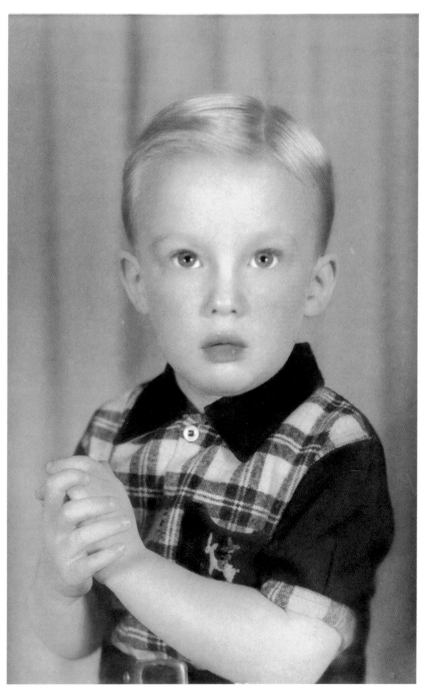

Even as a kid, I was thinking big, daydreaming of Trump towers.

My confirmation photo. That's me in the back, second from the right.

Here I am with my mother at the New York Military Academy. The discipline I learned there has benefited me all my life.

From an early age, my
beautiful daughter Iva
enjoyed black tie even

Proud dad and kids:
Ivanka, Don Jr., and Eric.

Now they're all grown up: Eric, Ivanka, and Don Jr.

The most fun I have is with my family. Here I am with my wife Melania and my youngest son Barron.

With my beautiful wife, Melania.

My daughter Tiffany is doing very well.

Getty Images

With Victoria and Joel Osteen, fantastic people.

One of the great things about my job is meeting many terrific people. Here I am with Piers Morgan, Joan Rivers, and Bret Michaels, all winners on *Celebrity Apprentice*.

I really enjoyed getting to know Sarah Palin.

Ronald Reagan is a political hero of mine. He took an America that appeared to be down and out and put us on top again.

Telling it like it is to George Stephanopoulos on *Good Morning America*.

Speaking at a Tea Party rally in Boca Raton, Florida.

What I do: erect the world's finest buildings, including the Trump World Tower at the United Nations Plaza.

40 Wall Street, the Trump Building, the tallest skyscraper in lower Manhattan.

Trump Tower and Trump International
Hotel and Tower in New York.

The West Side Rail Yards in New York City, also known as Trump Place, which I built with Chinese partners.

I own a large chunk of 1290 Avenue of the Americas in New York and the Bank of America building in San Francisco—thanks to the Chinese. Cost: zero.

The Great Dunes of Scotland. Trump International Golf Links, Aberdeen, Scotland.

The Trump National Golf Club, Washington, DC. Incredible property on the Potomac River.

Doing a firing on *The Apprentice*.

make: kill him with a missile or kill him in a raid. He made the decision, either of which would have been okay, and Osama bin Laden is dead.

It's wonderful that we got him, but what sane person would have decided otherwise? Why does Obama get so much credit? I know that's not politically correct to say, but if somebody can explain that to me, I would be very grateful. Our military deserves all the credit, not Obama.

Obama's violations of these seven principles are bad enough, but they are much worse when you consider the epic foreign policy failures he has committed in his first three years in office. Most Americans have been so focused on all of Barack Obama's economic failures and the disastrous effects of the Obama economy that they haven't had the time to pay close attention to how much he's screwed up America's national security. But a closer look uncovers some alarming realities.

⋖⋗

A commander in chief has to possess the right instincts. That's one of the biggest problems with Obama: his national security instincts are almost always wrong. On the campaign trail in 2008, Obama promised he would shut down the terrorist detention facility at Guantanamo Bay, Cuba. Then he got elected president, met the grown-ups in the military and intelligence worlds, and was forced to come to grips with the reality that Guantanamo serves a purpose, just as President George W. Bush and Vice President Dick Cheney maintained all along.

Then there was Obama's foolish instinct to treat terrorists as criminals (instead of the enemy combatants they are), giving them civilian trials rather than military tribunals. As everyone knows, civilian trials don't give prosecutors the latitude they need to put away dangerous terrorists and keep the country safe. But Obama and his attorney general, Eric Holder, thought otherwise. That is, until reality smacked them in the face again. Case in point was the painful education Obama got when Ahmed Ghailani was acquitted of more than 224 counts of murder in a civilian court for his part in the U.S. embassy bombings in Africa. "It was a near disaster," said Texas Republican Congressman Lamar Smith. "If Ghailani had been acquitted of just one more count, he would have been considered innocent of these heinous crimes."[3]

The blunder was reminiscent of Obama and Holder's asinine foot-dragging on whether to hold the trial of 9-11 mastermind Khalid Sheikh Mohammed in New York City of all places. Why Obama and Eric Holder would want to give one of America's biggest enemies a public relations platform and the biggest media megaphone in the world at the site of the Twin Tower terrorist attacks is beyond comprehension. But after a year of bumbling and tons of international humiliation, Obama and Holder finally decided to do what every clear-thinking American wanted to do in the first place, which was to try Khalid Sheikh Mohammed at Guantanamo.

Then there is Obama's recent decision to gut the U.S. military by cutting $400 billion from our defense budget, a figure more than double what then-Secretary of Defense Robert Gates identified as being prudent. Now here's Obama, a guy who never met a spending bill he doesn't love and one who has blown through more deficit spending than all presidents in 225 years combined. But when it comes to funding our troops and giving them the equipment, training, and support they need, Obama is MIA. As former Defense Secretary Gates said when he heard about his boss's brainless decision, such a move would degrade "force structure and military capability."[4]

Here's the deal: when your secretary of defense tells you that your proposed cuts will erode America's military capability, you pay attention. But not Obama. He thinks he knows how to run the military better than the guns in the fight. He's wrong. The reason conservatives support a strong and well-funded military is because they know that all freedoms flow from national security. That's why we need a new president. It's also why we need to get tough in foreign policy to deal with the threats and challenges America faces from rival and enemy nations.

CHINA

Even as Obama is busy degrading our military might by slashing the defense budget by a crippling $400 billion, the Communist Chinese are laughing their heads off and using the billions they make off us each year to jack up their military spending by 13 percent—*every year for the last twenty years!*[5]

Of course, because China's leadership is sneaky and underhanded, they significantly underreport their actual defense budget and technological advancement. It's actually part of their culture. As I mentioned earlier, they follow the words of Premier Deng who said China must "hide our capacities and bide our time." So they lie about their military spending and downplay their military sophistication every chance they get. For example, China claims its defense budget is just $78.6 billion a year. The Pentagon, however, believes the real number is over $150 billion. And when you factor in the purchasing power parity exchange rate, the real

Chinese military budget is closer to $300 billion (the second largest in the world)—an amount that is identical to the amount they rip us off every single year.[6]

China is also a master at head faking us when it comes to their weapons development. After the head of the People's Liberation Army (PLA) delegation, General Chen Bingde, visited America's National Defense University, he said, "To be honest, I feel very sad after visiting, because I think I feel, and I know how poor our equipments are and how underdeveloped we remain."[7] Only a fool would fall for such garbage. As the *Wall Street Journal* has reported, "Beijing has the most ambitious missile program in the world—including an anti-ship ballistic missile that threatens U.S. aircraft carriers."[8] We also know that China is busy building a fleet of nuclear submarines so large that it will soon overtake ours in size, is planning to build numerous aircraft carriers, and has significantly ramped up its cyberwarfare program and anti-satellite weapons. "If the United States can light a fire in China's backyard," said Colonel Dai Xu of the PLA, "we can also light a fire in their backyard."[9]

Then, in 2011, just one week before Chinese President Hu Jintao visited America, the PLA successfully tested its new stealth fighter jet, the J-20, an advanced medium bomber that the Obama administration thought the Chinese were still years away from flying.[10] As one defense expert put it, "It was a middle-finger welcome salute to Defense Secretary Robert Gates,"[11] who was then in China on an official visit. And what did Obama do? Not wanting to mess up his chance to bow down to yet *another* foreign leader, the president did what he always does when our enemies take a swipe at us—nothing. Instead, he let Hu Jintao waltz into our country the very next week and make a total joke out of us and showcase Barack Obama's weakness. Worse, Obama groveled at the feet of the Communist he depends on to loan him the money to fund our president's disastrous spending programs. As Hillary Clinton put it privately, "How do you deal toughly with your banker?"[12]

Here's my answer: you wake up and realize that money is *itself* a weapon. Hu Jintao gets that. Most Americans get that. But the clueless bunch in the White House seems not to understand that, or maybe they just don't care. Either way, the Communist Chinese know that collecting our debt allows them to hold us hostage with the threat that they will dump our debt and send interest rates skyrocketing. That's also why China is snatching up minerals, oil, and food in Africa, South America, and the Middle East.[13] When you combine this economic "weaponry" with China's aggressive military buildup, it's crystal clear that America should be strengthening our military muscle, not weakening it. Specifically, defense experts believe that meeting China's military challenge will require that we deploy more submarines, more 5th generation aircraft like the F-22 Raptor and F-35 Lightning, bolster our anti-submarine and anti-mining capabilities, add missile and cruise-missile defense systems, beef up our cyber-warfare technologies, sharpen our reconnaissance platforms, and add longer-range precision-strike platforms.[14] Will Barack Obama do those things? Fat chance. We need a president who will.

RUSSIA

Obama's popularity in America may be at rock bottom levels, but I know one place his ratings are likely sky high: the Kremlin. Russia's leaders can hardly believe their luck. Never in a million years did they think

America would elect a guy as ineffective as this. Obama's pretty-please diplomacy and endless American apology tours have served Russian interests extremely well. Russian Prime Minister Vladimir Putin, of whom I often speak highly for his intelligence and no-nonsense way, is a former KGB officer. No sooner did Obama move into 1600 Pennsylvania Avenue than he began making concessions and sacrificing American power on the altar of "improving relations" with Russia.

According to Barack Obama's favorite newspaper, the *New York Times*, within weeks of being sworn in as president of the United States, Obama sent a top U.S. official to Moscow to hand deliver a secret letter to Russia's then-President Dmitry Medvedev. According to the *Times*, the secret letter said that Obama "would back off deploying a new missile defense system in Eastern Europe if Moscow would help stop Iran from developing long-range weapons." It's so outrageous I hardly believed it until I read it myself. Obama had barely moved his stuff into the White House residence and already the guy was just *itching* to start degrading America's power and undermining our allies.

Not surprisingly, Putin was ecstatic: "The latest decision by President Obama...has positive implications," said Putin. "I very much hope that this very right and brave decision will be followed by others."[15]

But it gets even worse. Incredibly, the Obama administration made the decision to throw our friends Poland and the Czech Republic under the bus and leave them naked to missile attacks "despite having no public guarantees" that Moscow would help crack down on Iran's missile programs.[16] Many in the intelligence world were baffled by Obama's reckless and foolish move. U.S. senators piped up too. "This is going to be seen as a capitulation to the Russians, who had no real basis to object to what we were doing," warned Republican Senator Lindsey Graham of South Carolina. "And at the end of the day you empowered the Russians, you made Iran happy and you made the people in Eastern Europe wonder who we are as Americans."[17] What was Barack Obama's response? "If the byproduct of it is that the Russians feel a little less paranoid and are now willing to work more effectively with us to deal with threats like ballistic missiles from Iran or nuclear development in Iran, you know, then that's a bonus."

The results of Obama's pandering to the Russians have been a total disaster. In 2010, the Russians outsmarted Obama by promising to play nice and not sell Iran anti-aircraft missiles. The administration proudly hailed the announcement as a big success and praised Medvedev for having "shown leadership in holding Iran accountable for its actions, from start to finish." Then, even as Obama was busy cheerleading the Russians' actions, the *Los Angeles Times* reported that "Russian diplomats were quietly recruiting other countries…to undercut tougher penalties imposed on the Islamic Republic."[18] It was an incredible coup for Russia: they got Obama to give up missile defense for absolutely nothing in return *and* stuck it to America by secretly convincing other nations to back Iran.

Putin has big plans for Russia. He wants to edge out its neighbors so that Russia can dominate oil supplies to all of Europe.[19] Putin has also announced his grand vision: the creation of a "Eurasian Union" made up of former Soviet nations that can dominate the region. I respect Putin and the Russians but cannot believe our leader allows them to get away with so much—I am sure that Vladimir Putin is even more surprised than I am. Hats off to the Russians.

IRAN

Obama's plan to have Russia stand up to Iran was a horrible failure that turned America into a laughingstock. Unfortunately, our current foreign policy toward Iran has been just as embarrassing and disastrous.

First, there was the epic and inexplicable failure of Obama to speak out strongly for freedom during Iran's so-called "Green Revolution." As the world watched, Iranian college kids and dissidents took to the streets to peacefully protest for democratic reforms and human rights, only to be violently suppressed by the regime's thugs. What did Obama do? As incredible and outrageous as it might seem, he sat silent. We're talking about an Iranian regime led by Mahmoud Ahmadinejad, a guy who has declared Iran's desire to see one of our greatest allies, Israel, "wiped off the map." But did Obama stand up for the voices of freedom and against the anti-Israel forces of Iran's Islamic Revolutionary Guard? Not a chance. Had Obama stepped out to help the protesters early, the regime could have easily been overthrown and we would not have our biggest problem today. When it comes to defending human rights in the Islamic world, Obama shies away because he thinks America should be apologizing to Muslim countries rather than speaking out. It's a disgrace.

The greatest outrage, however, has been Obama's unwillingness to stand strong in the face of Ahmadinejad's nuclear weapon ambitions. Iran is the most sanctioned member of the United Nations. Since 2006, Iran has been the focus of five Security Council resolutions demanding that it stop its uranium enrichment.[20] And yet, knowing all this, Obama continues to concoct his kindergarten-style "solutions" for dealing with the Iranian threat. For example, even as the adults in the intelligence world are wracking their brains about how to stop Iran from developing an operational nuclear weapon, Barack Obama proposed something so childish I'm almost embarrassed to write about it. Obama wanted to create a telephone hotline between America and Iran. I kid you not. Obama's solution to thwarting a nuclear Iran is to set up a little telephone line that our military can use to talk nicely with the Iranian terrorist regime that threatens to destroy America.

As pathetic and ridiculous as that is, here's the most humiliating part: Iran laughed at him and rejected the plan outright. Worse, once they heard Obama's proposal and realized what a joke the guy is, they were emboldened to get tough. "In addition to rejecting the hot line," reported the *Wall Street Journal*, "Iranian military officers have threatened to deploy Iranian naval forces in the Western Hemisphere, including potentially the *Gulf of Mexico*"[21] (emphasis mine).

How did the White House respond? Obama sent his press secretary out with this message of strength: "We don't take these statements seriously, given that they do not reflect at all Iran's naval capabilities."[22] How reassuring!

The point isn't that Iran's navy is incapable of anchoring its ships off the coast of Florida. The point is that Iran's government has so little fear, so little respect for America's leadership, that it feels free to make the threat. The Iranians know our president will sit back and do nothing, just like he did during Iran's Green Revolution. They know Obama's instincts are to apologize, grovel, and retreat. As the *Wall Street Journal* pointed out, "Tehran appears to be taking a more aggressive posture in the Persian Gulf, in part as a response to the scheduled drawdown of American forces in Iraq and Afghanistan."[23] In other words, because Obama made the horrible

decision to announce a date of withdrawal, Iran now feels emboldened to
throw its weight around. By the way, in 2011, U.S. defense officials reported
that there have been several "near-misses" between Islamic Revolutionary
Guards Corps (IRGC) speed boats challenging U.S. and allied war ships.[24]
Way to go, Mr. President.

America's primary goal with Iran must be to destroy its nuclear ambitions. Let me put this as plainly as I know how: Iran's nuclear program
must be stopped—by any and all means necessary. Period. We cannot
allow this radical regime to acquire a nuclear weapon that they will either
use or hand off to terrorists. Better now than later!

At the end of his second term, President George W. Bush authorized a
covert program to "undermine the electrical and computer systems" at
Natanz, Iran's uranium enrichment facility.[25] What came out of that initiative was the creation of the world's most advanced cyber-weapon ever. With
technical support from Israel, as well as technology from other allies, the
Stuxnet cyber worm was unleashed against Iran's nuclear centrifuges and
made them spin so fast they destroyed themselves. The operation was very
successful and destroyed roughly one-fifth of Iran's centrifuges. No one
knows for sure how many months or years we put back on Iran's nuclear
clock. Some analysts say six months, others one or two years. But that's the
point: the clock is still ticking.

Many experts believe the only way to eliminate the Iranian nuclear
threat is to bomb their facilities. Israel has used airstrikes to knock out
nuclear facilities twice: once in 1981 on an Iraqi nuclear site, and again in
2007 to destroy a nuclear bomb plant in Syria. It's clear that Iran is prepar-

ing itself for this possibility. In September 2011, Iran moved its most important nuclear fuel production to a "heavily defended underground military
facility" to guard their supplies from a possible air or cyber-attack. The
White House spokesman for the National Security Council said the move
was a direct violation of the UN security requirements and was "another
provocative act."[26] But, as usual, Obama will do nothing. He's too busy
trying to get reelected, going to fundraisers, and vacationing.

Worse, we know Obama's instincts on Iran are horrible. On May 18,
2008, during a campaign speech then-candidate Obama made this breath-
takingly ignorant statement: "I mean, think about it. Iran, Cuba, Venezuela—these countries are tiny, compared to the Soviet Union. They don't
pose a serious threat to us the way the Soviet Union posed a threat to us.…
You know, Iran, they spend one-one hundredth of what we spend on the
military. If Iran ever tried to pose a serious threat to us, they wouldn't stand
a chance. And we should use that position of strength that we have, to be
bold enough to go ahead and listen." Then, after his advisors told him what
a moronic statement he'd made, Obama went out two days later and
reversed his stance: "Iran is a grave threat. It has an illicit nuclear program,
it supports terrorism across the region and militias in Iraq, it threatens
Israel's existence, it denies the holocaust."[27] Once again, the guy's initial
instincts are always wrong. And in this case, they endangered America and
our ally Israel.

Obviously we must listen to our intelligence experts to decide the best
way to thwart Iran's nuclear ambitions. But here's the reality: because the
clock is ticking down, the next president America elects will in all likelihood

be the president who either stops Iran from obtaining a nuclear weapon or who sits back and lets it happen. Given Obama's track record of weakness, that's not a risk America can afford to take.

PAKISTAN

When our tremendous Navy SEALS took out Osama bin Laden, they didn't find him in some obscure hole in the ground or in a remote mountainside cave. No, they found him in Pakistan right next door to one of Pakistan's most prestigious military academies. What does that tell you? It tells me that Pakistan knew where Osama was all along.

Get it straight: Pakistan is not our friend. We've given them billions and billions of dollars, and what did we get? Betrayal and disrespect—and much worse. When one of our helicopters was downed during the Osama bin Laden raid, Pakistan handed it over to China so that Chinese engineers could study it and steal the technology we spent billions of dollars developing. The Pakistanis think we're a bunch of dopes. They don't respect us and they never will as long as Obama is our commander in chief. And it's much, much worse than just disrespect. In May 2011, Pakistan actually fired on American Apache helicopter crews. As one military official stated, "We're not allowed to return fire to coordinates inside the Pakistan border. We know it's the Pakistani military in many cases. Pakistan has been instigating."[28]

The fact that our rules of engagement (ROE) don't allow our military to defend themselves and return fire is absolute lunacy. We need to remove the handcuffs and get tough. You shoot at our troops, our troops shoot at you. End of story.

But there's an even graver threat emerging out of Pakistan. I'm talking about the rise of the so-called Haqqani Network, a terrorist network estimated to be 15,000 fighters strong. The Haqquani Network is closely allied with al Qaeda. The Haqqanis originated in Afghanistan but have now holed up in Pakistan. They are considered bigger and better funded than al Qaeda. Here's the worst part: Pakistan's Inter-Services Intelligence (ISI) is helping the Haqqanis. Former chairman of the Joint Chiefs of Staff Admiral Michael Mullen has worked closer with Pakistan than most. He says that the Haqqani Network has become "a strategic arm" of Pakistan's intelligence agency and is responsible for the attacks on the U.S. embassy in Kabul, the Inter-Continental Hotel in Kabul, and the truck bomb attack that injured seventy-seven U.S. soldiers.[29]

And get this: according to intelligence experts, "Pakistan is preparing to replace the billions of dollars of critical military aid it has been receiving from the U.S. by courting China and soliciting help from Islamic ally Saudi Arabia."[30]

When are we going to wake up and realize that we are funding our enemies? And when are we going to let our troops hit back? Right now we ban our forces from using Predator drones inside the city of Miram where the Haqqanis are headquartered. The reason? Obama didn't want to "offend" the Pakistanis. That's absurd—they're killing our soldiers! We need to get tough, give our troops permission to return fire, and tell Pakistan that we will sever all economic activity with them until they cut ties with the Haqqani network. If the Pakistani intelligence services work with terrorists, we should declare their military a terrorist organization.[31]

LIBYA

Obama ran for president on a platform that he wouldn't start any more "illegal wars." Guess what? He started an "illegal war." He never went before Congress to ask for a declaration of war with Libya. Instead, Obama launched one by himself and thrust America into a bloody civil war. Isn't that what Obama bashed George W. Bush for doing, even though Bush got rid of Saddam Hussein?

Now Qaddafi is dead and gone. So what? We have spent more than $1 billion on the Libya operation. And what are we getting in return? A huge bill, that's what. It's incredible how foolish the Obama administration is. Libya has enormous oil reserves. When the so-called "rebels" came to NATO (which is really the U.S.) and asked for help to defeat Qaddafi, we should have said, "Sure, we don't like the guy either. We will help you take out Qaddafi. But in exchange, you give us 50 percent of your oil for the next twenty-five years to pay for our military support and to say thank you for the United States doing what you could never have done on your own." The "rebels" would have jumped at the offer and said yes. After all, they didn't stand a chance—they were being routed—it was over. But did we do that? No. Our leaders are too brainless to negotiate a deal like that.

Imagine the amount of oil we could have secured for America. Think about how much economic relief we would have secured for our people and our businesses. A deal like that would have been so easy to broker. But our diplomats are pansies. They don't want to "offend" anyone. Guess what? The American people are offended! Our policy should be: no oil, no military support. No exceptions.

Even with Qaddafi gone now, unfortunately, the price we will pay for our stupid Libyan policy may end up being far more expensive and dire than the billion dollars we've already blown there. In September 2011, up to 20,000 shoulder-fired anti-aircraft missiles went missing in Libya. According to the left-leaning group Human Rights Watch, the reason this happened was because Barack Obama refused to provide proper protection to guard the weapons stockpiles.[32] When weapons went missing in Iraq, the liberal media made a massive story out of it and used the issue to try and defeat George W. Bush. But now, on Obama's watch, 20,000 shoulder-fired missiles—the kind that can take down a commercial jetliner—are nowhere to be found, and the mainstream media yawns.

There's no telling how much money those missiles will be sold for on the black market. But there's one thing you can bet your bottom dollar on, and that's every terrorist organization will be standing in line to buy them. We know that al Qaeda is already in Libya. Former White House counterterrorism advisor Richard Clark says that the probability of al Qaeda successfully smuggling the missiles out of Libya is "pretty high."[33] When the story surfaced, as usual, the White House shrugged its shoulders. "We have…worked closely with the [Libyan rebel leaders] as well as NATO in investigating and dealing with the issue of conventional weapons in Libya," said Press Secretary Jay Carney. "We are exploring every option to expand our support."[34]

Nice!

Now here's the worst of it: guess who "discreetly" provided the Libyan rebels with "humanitarian aid" before the fall of Libya's capital, Tripoli? That's right: Iran. When the rebels seized the capital, Iran "congratulated the Muslim people of Libya."[35]

Like everyone else, I'm glad Qaddafi is gone. But if we had been smart and negotiated shrewdly, we would have taken 50 percent of Libya's oil for twenty-five years before we spent mountains of American money. Once again, Obama has proven to be a horrible negotiator and an expert at missing huge opportunities for America. And guess who gets much of that oil from Libya—that's right, it's China, not the U.S.

⇒·⇐

Americans have been too busy fighting the ravages of the Obama economy to notice what a colossal disaster the community organizer has been as our commander in chief. The damage Obama has done to our military and to our standing in the world can only be repaired by electing a new president, one who respects our men and women in uniform and pursues a national security doctrine that puts America first.

SEVEN

A SAFETY NET,
NOT A HAMMOCK

*Continued dependence upon relief induces a spiritual
and moral disintegration fundamentally destructive to the
national fiber. To dole out relief in this way is to administer
a narcotic, a subtle destroyer of the human spirit.
It is inimical to the dictates of sound policy.
It is in violation of the traditions of America.*

**—President Franklin Delano Roosevelt,
1935 State of the Union**

In 1964, President Lyndon Baines Johnson declared "War on Poverty."
Guess what? Poverty won. Big time.

Since Johnson launched his mythical quest for a government-run
utopia, welfare spending has skyrocketed 13 times the amount spent in
1964 (in inflation adjusted dollars). Back then, welfare spending accounted
for 1.2 percent of GDP. Today, it's almost 6 percent.[1] That means taxpayers
have paid—are you ready for this?—a jaw-dropping $16 trillion on public-
assistance programs.[2] That's a totally outrageous sum—until you realize
what Obama wants to spend over the next decade.

In 2011, Obama jacked welfare spending up 42 percent over 2008 levels. This huge increase means America is paying $953 billion a year on welfare.[3] America is flat broke. We cannot afford to spend $10 trillion over the next decade on dependency-inducing welfare schemes that have created an underclass, demoralized it, and drained taxpayers who are paying for programs that not only make poverty worse but that are notoriously rife with fraud and abuse.

You want an example? In 2010, the *Los Angeles Times* reported that welfare recipients in California were using their welfare cards to get cash from ATMs at strip clubs. Taxpayers should not be paying for some guy's lap dance![4] And over in Virginia, taxpayers were outraged when it was revealed that their tax dollars were going to subsidize welfare recipients living in luxury apartments, complete with "resort-style swimming pools with fountains and heated spas, billiard rooms, granite counter tops, indoor basketball courts, and stainless steel appliances." "These are resort-style amenities that the majority of the taxpayers that are subsidizing it don't have in their own [homes]," said supervisor Pat Herrity. "Luxury has no place in subsidized housing."[5]

Look, I believe deeply that America must maintain a sturdy safety net. We have an obligation to take care of those who can't take care of themselves, whether due to age or illness. Our country has a big heart. And it's a point of national pride that we take care of our own. It's one of the things that makes us so great. And certainly our people need a lot more help given that President Obama has been such a total disaster. Today, under this administration, more people than ever in America's history—a staggering 46.2 million—live under the federal poverty line. Many of these individuals are out of work. They need temporary assistance as they search for the few jobs that remain in the Obama economy. We should help these folks and their kids, no question about it. But it is counterproductive and cruel to allow America's safety net to morph into a hammock. It is simply immoral for the government to encourage able-bodied Americans to think that a life on welfare, of being supported by taxpayers, is an acceptable lifestyle.

Our Founding Fathers understood that self-reliance is the axis on which freedom spins. The American work ethic is what led generations of Americans to create our once prosperous nation. The idea that working hard was a spiritual act of doing one's work "as unto the Lord" spurred us to give our very best day in and day out. And because we believed that work was a virtue, we produced massive wealth, plentiful jobs, and a self-sufficient society.

That's what I find so morally offensive about welfare dependency: it robs people of the chance to improve. Work gives every day a sense of purpose. A job well done provides a sense of pride and accomplishment. I love to work. In fact, I like working so much that I seldom take vacations. Because I work so hard, I've been privileged to create jobs for tens of thousands of people. And on my hit show *The Apprentice*, I get to work with people from all walks of life. I'm known for my famous line, "You're fired!" But the truth is, I don't like firing people. Sometimes you have to do it, but it's never fun or easy. One of my favorite parts of business is seeing how work transforms people into better, more confident, more competent individuals. It's inspiring and beautiful to watch.

America became a powerhouse because of our deep belief in the virtue of self-reliance. As Thomas Jefferson said, "I predict future happiness for

Americans if they can prevent the government from wasting the labors of the people under the pretense of taking care of them." Government wasn't created to take care of us. Generations of Americans believed they should be responsible for themselves. When hard times hit, churches and neighbors pitched in and pulled together to help. But in the end, the Founders believed that government should only do those few things individuals couldn't do for themselves. We are rapidly losing that self-reliant spirit that made America great.

Proper Perspective on Poverty

Real economic pain exists in America. No doubt about that. And we need pro-growth, pro-jobs policies. But it's also important for us not to lose sight of the bigger picture. Obama tries to justify his massive spending programs in part based on the idea that they're needed to eradicate poverty in America, but as Dinesh D'Souza, author of the bestselling book *What's So Great about America*, points out, America is one of the few places in the world where a "poor" person can still be obese.[6] "Poor" is a relative term. By global standards, poor people in America are rich. And even by American standards, poor people today are better off than average people were in our parents' lifetimes. According to a Heritage Foundation study, "Today, poor boys at ages 18 and 19 are actually taller and heavier than boys of similar age in the general U.S. population in the late 1950s. They are one inch taller and some 10 pounds heavier than GIs of similar age during World War II."[7]

Poor people in America have comforts most of the world's poor have never seen, as the Heritage Foundation reports:

- 80 percent of poor households have air conditioning. In 1970, only 36 percent of the entire U.S. population enjoyed air conditioning.
- 92 percent of poor households have a microwave.
- Nearly three-fourths have a car or truck, and 31 percent have two or more cars or trucks.
- Nearly two-thirds have cable or satellite TV.
- Two-thirds have at least one DVD player, and 70 percent have a VCR.
- Half have a personal computer, and one in seven have two or more computers.
- More than half of poor families with children have a video game system, such as an Xbox or PlayStation.
- 43 percent have Internet access.
- One-third have a wide-screen plasma or LCD TV.
- One-fourth have a digital video recorder system, such as a TiVo.[8]

Does this mean that poor Americans aren't in need of help, most especially a job? No, of course not. But it does mean that Americans should never lose sight of the fact that we are incredibly blessed to live in a nation where 97 percent of those considered poor own a color television and have the electricity to power it.[9]

Childhood Poverty Is a Tragedy

The innocent bystanders of American poverty are kids. Yet two-thirds of childhood poverty in America is absolutely preventable if individuals did just one thing: get married before they have children. As someone once put it, "Marriage is the greatest 'anti-poverty' program God ever created."

An out-of-wedlock child is six times more likely to live in poverty than a child born in a two-parent home. The reason for this is painfully obvious: two paychecks are twice as much as one. This isn't brain surgery. Two people working full-time at Walmart puts a family above the federal poverty line (defined as a family of four earning less than $22,314, not including in-kind benefits). The key thing is for the father to stick around, which is what marriage is meant to ensure. Both parents don't necessarily have to hold down a job. One paycheck from a gainfully employed dad, with mom at home taking care of the kids, is better than a single mother living off welfare.

The explosion of out-of-wedlock births in America is staggering. This is a total departure from American history—one that is reshaping our country, and not for the better. Back when LBJ began engineering his "Great Society" and declaring his "War on Poverty," only 7 percent of kids were born out of wedlock. Today, 40 percent of all births in America are to unwed mothers. Government is now the "father" in far too many homes. But here's the thing: kids don't just need a wallet—they need a dad who will teach boys how to be responsible men and show daughters what it means to be respected and protected.

Out-of-wedlock birth rates are not only one of the greatest generators of poverty but of inequality in America. Twenty-nine percent of white children are born to a single mother (a figure that's far too high), but 72 percent of black children are born out of wedlock. Beyond the economic consequences, we know that kids without a dad are also exponentially more likely to abuse drugs, drop out of school, commit crime, and be incarcerated.[10] Kids who grow up in homes where a magic check appears each month from the government believe there's nothing wrong with sitting at home doing nothing while taxpayers bust their humps working to fund them. For an entire generation, government welfare programs are eradicating the virtues of responsibility, hard work, and self-reliance that built America.

Luis Lopez is a Democrat and youth counselor in Florida. He tells the story of an exchange he had with a 13-year-old pregnant girl he met in an inner-city, low-income housing project. He asked who was going to pay for her baby. Smiling, she said, "Medicaid and Social Security will pay for it." "What about the father?" "We broke up," she said. The girl went on to explain that her grandmother would raise her child. Then Lopez asked the pregnant teen what her mom thought about the fact that she was so young and pregnant. "My mom had me when she was 14," the girl replied. "So what's the problem?"[11]

It wasn't always this way. A lot of us remember a time when there was a social stigma and sense of shame against living on the public dole. There's a great scene in the movie *Cinderella Man* with Russell Crowe that illustrates how radically our entitlement culture has changed America. The movie is based on the true story of boxer James J. Braddock, a fighter during the Great Depression who goes on to become heavyweight champion of the world. As Braddock struggles to establish his boxing career, he eventually has to turn to public assistance to feed his wife and kids. He's deeply embarrassed and ashamed, but he has no other options, so he accepts the money. Later, as his boxing career takes off and the prize money starts rolling in, Braddock returns to the welfare office and stands in line patiently. When he reaches the front of the line, he hands the welfare worker a stack of cash to pay back the government the money he had received to support his kids. That really happened. But today, given our entitlement culture, we can hardly imagine something like that except in the movies.

We have to combat the welfare mentality that says individuals are entitled to live off taxpayers. We need to reaffirm that mothers and fathers have a responsibility to their children—and that it starts with getting married before they have them. But unfortunately our welfare system has created monetary incentives to avoid marriage and to have more out-of-wedlock children in order to get bigger welfare benefits. Each year, taxpayers shell out $300 billion to unmarried parents.[12] That's almost a third of a trillion dollars that could easily be saved if we could restore personal responsibility and the importance of marriage before childbearing. Your tax dollars in the form of Medicaid also pick up the delivery costs for 40 percent of all children born in America, most of those children being born to never-married mothers.[13]

For too many of these mothers and their children, living off welfare becomes a way of life. Consider these numbers: since becoming president, Obama has added 8 million more Americans to the rolls,[14] and food stamp spending has more than doubled since 2007, going from $33 billion to $77 billion.[15] But even more shocking than these figures is that half of food stamps go to people who have been on public assistance for eight and a half years or more.[16] The only good thing about this for Obama, and he knows it…they will all be voting for him.

Obama's "Food Stamp Crime Wave"

The food stamp program was originally created as temporary assistance for families with momentary times of need. And it shouldn't be needed often. Thankfully, 96 percent of America's poor parents say their children never suffer even a day of hunger.[17] But when half of food stamp recipients have been on the dole for nearly a decade, something is clearly wrong, and some of it has to do with fraud.

The *Wall Street Journal* has reported that Obama's food stamp policies are ushering in a massive "food stamp crime wave."[18] That's been matched by fewer prosecutions of illegal food stamp transactions involving alcohol or other non-eligible items.[19] And "millionaires are now legally entitled to collect food stamps as long as they have little or no monthly income."[20]

As the *Wall Street Journal* notes, "The Obama administration is far more enthusiastic about boosting food-stamp enrollment than about preventing fraud." Under Obama's rapid expansion of food stamps, recipients are selling welfare benefit cards on Facebook and Craigslist and using the money to buy drugs,[21] food stamp checks are going to prison inmates,[22] a $2 million lottery winner qualified for food stamps (and complained that he still deserved food stamps because the government took half his winnings in taxes),[23] and the program is rife with incredibly costly scams including one enterprising crook who created more than 1,000 fraudulent food stamp claims and pocketed $8 million.[24] And that's just scratching the surface of the program's waste, fraud, and abuse. The really infuriating thing is that the Obama administration doesn't seem to care about how taxpayers are being shaken down by this outrageously mismanaged government program.

The blatant waste of taxpayers' dollars doesn't bother Obama, because it's all part of his broader nanny-state agenda. It seems he believes the more voters he gives welfare goodies to, the more votes he'll rack up for reelection. Perhaps that's why his administration doesn't give a rip about policing fraud or administering responsible oversight—he's buying votes! And like any good leftist knows, the bigger you grow the welfare state, the bigger you grow your electoral army. It's an outrageous betrayal of the American taxpayer and of the twin pillars of hard work and self-reliance that support the American Dream of freedom, progress, and bettering oneself and one's family.

We see the same trend in public housing, where since Barack Obama's election, massive crowds have been lining up to get Section 8 housing. In Atlanta, for example, 30,000 people showed up in the hopes of getting government housing applications or vouchers.[25] There's no doubt that some of those individuals are truly in need, whether due to age or disability, but the fact is that we know that able-bodied, non-elderly individuals without children routinely enter the program and spend on average nearly eight years in public housing.[26] That's outrageous.

People who have the ability to work should. But with the government happy to send checks, too many of them don't. On average, able-bodied welfare recipients work just sixteen hours a *week*. How can anyone expect to climb out of poverty working just over three hours a day in a five-day work week?[27] More hours at work equals more income. But our government's welfare trap has built a system that creates a disincentive for work. The more hours you work the fewer welfare goodies you get. So what do you think people are going to do? They keep their work hours artificially low to keep their welfare checks artificially high. And once again, America's twin virtues of hard work and self-reliance take a beating.

When you realize that every seventh person you pass on the sidewalk now receives food stamps, and that Obama has upped welfare spending to just under $1 trillion a year, it becomes painfully clear that this president's rapid expansion of the welfare industry is part of a much broader effort to "fundamentally transform America," as Obama put it early in his presidency.

I've got a newsflash for you, Mr. President: America likes America the way the Founding Fathers built her—as a nation that deeply values hard work and self-reliance. The next president America elects must be committed to serious welfare reforms that overhaul the system and roll back Obama's disastrous public assistance policies.

We know how to reform welfare because we've done it before. In 1996, then-Speaker Newt Gingrich and congressional Republicans passed and pushed President Clinton to sign the 1996 Welfare Reform Act. In the wake of the bill's passage, the liberal *New York Times* ran a breathless op-ed with the headline: "A Sad Day for Poor Children." "This is not reform, it is punishment," read the article. "The effect on cities will be devastating."[28] As usual, the *New York Times* could not have been more wrong. The results were as dramatic as they were hopeful: welfare caseloads went down 60 percent, 2.8 million families transitioned from welfare to work, and 1.6 million kids climbed out of poverty.[29]

Welfare to Work

The secret to the 1996 Welfare Reform Act's success was that it tied welfare to work. To get your check, you had to prove that you were enrolled in job-training or trying to find work. But here's the rub: the 1996 Welfare Reform Act only dealt with one program, Aid to Families with Dependent Children (AFDC), not the other seventy-six welfare programs which, today, cost taxpayers more than $900 billion annually.[30] We need to take a page from the 1996 reform and do the same for other welfare programs. Benefits should have strings attached to them. After all, if it's our money recipients are getting, we the people should have a say in how it's spent.

The way forward is to do what we did with AFDC and attach welfare benefits to work. The Welfare Reform Act of 2011—proposed by Republican Congressmen Jim Jordan of Ohio, Tim Scott of South Carolina, and Scott Garrett of New Jersey—does just that.[31] Their bill, if enacted, would make sure that welfare programs would serve only those who truly need them, place a cap on welfare expenditures to prevent bureaucrats from endlessly expanding the programs, give more authority to the states over welfare spending, prevent federal funding of abortions through welfare programs, and enforce work requirements, among other reforms. [32] It's a serious plan that deserves to be passed and signed into law.

Of course, just as with the 1996 Welfare Reform Act, liberals will cry, kick, scream, and throw temper tantrums. But let them. It's far more important that we help poor people to become independent, self-sufficient individuals who gain the benefits of work. Let's get it done.

Next, I believe that the state of Florida made a smart move when in 2011 it became the only state to require drug testing of all recipients of the welfare program Temporary Assistance to Needy Families (TANF). As Florida Governor Rick Scott said, "While there are certainly legitimate needs for public assistance, it is unfair for Florida taxpayers to subsidize drug addiction. This new law will encourage personal accountability and will help to prevent the misuse of tax dollars."[33] The governor is right. It's common sense. By the way, Rick Scott is doing a great job and not getting the credit he deserves.

Look, millions of employees have to get drug tested for their jobs. Do they make a big stink about it? No. It's only smart. But leave it to the know-nothings at the American Civil Liberties Union (ACLU) to whine and cry about a requirement that millions of hard-working taxpayers go through year in and year out. "The wasteful program created by this law subjects Floridians who are impacted by the economic downturn, as well as their families, to a humiliating search of their urine and body fluids," said a foolish Howard Simon, executive director of ACLU Florida.[34] Humiliating? Excuse me? How is it "humiliating" to make sure that taxpayers aren't funding a drug addict's next hit? And how is it "humiliating" to take a drug screen that millions of working people take with no problem? It's not.

It's just one more example of liberals' attempting to erode personal responsibility and waste taxpayers' money.

The bill requires that TANF recipients take and pass a drug test. If it's a two-parent household, both individuals get tested. Anyone who tests positive for drugs is ineligible for benefits for a year. If they fail it a second time they are ineligible for three years. Recipients cover the cost of the screening, which they later recoup through benefits.[35] If parents fail the drug test, benefits for children can be awarded to a third-party recipient acting as a guardian provided he or she passes a drug test.[36]

This common sense approach should be a no-brainer. It's insane to ask taxpayers to foot the bill for some junkie's drug habit when America is already $15 trillion in the hole and many Americans are fighting to survive in the Obama economy. Bottom line: you do drugs, no welfare check. End of story.

Finally, it's time to get tough on those who cheat and defraud taxpayers. The Obama-fueled welfare "crime wave" must end fast. Otherwise, it will further spread the mindset that says, "Who cares if I cheat the system, it's not my money. I deserve free stuff." That means punishing violators, not turning a blind eye like the Obama administration has done. And that includes punishing corrupt bureaucrats who run scams and leave taxpayers holding the bill. Also, no more millionaires getting welfare checks. That's outrageous and must be stopped immediately.

⟨⟩

America has a big heart. We believe in helping our fellow citizens when they are down on their luck, become seriously disabled, or reach an age when they can't care for themselves. For those folks, the safety net is necessary and totally appropriate.

Yet for too many people, welfare has become a way of life. There's nothing "compassionate" about allowing welfare dependency to be passed from generation to generation. Kids deserve better. America deserves better.

President Reagan put it best: "Welfare's purpose should be to eliminate, as far as possible, the need for its own existence."

EIGHT

REPEAL OBAMACARE

We have to pass the bill so that you
can find out what is in it.

—Former Speaker Nancy Pelosi,
March 9, 2010

Former Speaker of the House Nancy Pelosi said Congress had to pass Obamacare so we could find out what's in it. Now we have. And what's inside those 2,733 pages is a job-killing, health care-destroying monstrosity. It can't be reformed, salvaged, or fixed. It's that bad. Obamacare has to be killed now before it grows into an even bigger mess, as it inevitably will. Obamacare takes full effect in 2014. If it's not repealed before then, it will be more than just another failed government entitlement program—it will be the trillion-ton weight that finally takes down our economy forever.

Polls show that more than 80 percent of Americans are reasonably pleased with their current health insurance plan.[1] That's an impressive number. Still, everyone agrees we need to take steps to reduce the rising costs of health care and make insurance more affordable. But socialized medicine is not the solution. That's why the majority of Americans are against Obamacare. They know that giving our inept, bumbling federal government control over health care is an invitation to disaster. Obamacare is a heat-seeking missile that will destroy jobs and small businesses; it will explode health-care costs; and it will lead to health care that is far less innovative than it is today. Every argument that you'd make against socialism you can make against socialized health care, and any candidate who isn't 100 percent committed to scrapping Obamacare is not someone America should elect president. Repealing Obamacare may be one of the most important and consequential actions our next president takes.

Obamacare Puts Small Businesses on Life Support

It's sad to see just how many citizens—some of them smart people—got duped into believing Obama's bait and switch sales pitch on Obamacare. Take, for instance, Starbucks CEO Howard Schultz. Schultz did a terrific job of turning Starbucks around. But when it came to Obamacare, he took the bait hook, line, and sinker. "When I was invited to the White House prior to health care being reformed, I was very supportive of the president's plan," Schultz said. However, after Schultz and his team studied the massive bill more closely, he changed his tune. "As the bill is currently written and if it was going to land in 2014 under the current guidelines, the pressure on small businesses, because of the [individual] mandate, is too great."[2]

That's putting it mildly. A September 2011 report by UBS, the highly respected financial services company, said, "Arguably the biggest impediment to hiring (particularly hiring of less skilled workers) is healthcare reform, which has the added drawback of straining state and federal budgets."[3] The report went on to explain in simple language why Obamacare is such a jobs killer:

> The new law requires most businesses to provide a generous "essential" package of benefits, which is beyond what many small businesses provide today. It subjects businesses to highly complex rules that increase the cost, risk, and "hassle factor" of adding to payrolls. Companies that do offer insurance can be fined if low-income employees take a government-subsidized plan. All firms with more than 50 workers must provide benefits, which creates an incentive for smaller firms to stay "under the limit" by expanding overseas, outsourcing, or dividing into two companies.[4]

And liberals scratch their heads and wonder why businesses don't want to hire?

Simple: companies know Obama is anti-business, and his government-run health-care takeover has created a major disincentive to hire new workers. So business leaders aren't hiring. Instead, they will just ship more jobs overseas or automate their systems with machines. Just do some simple math. If you have a business with fifty employees, would you hire that fatal fifty-first employee and instantly subject yourself to a $100,000+

penalty ($2,000 for every employee in your company) for having the audacity to create more jobs, enlarge your business, and stimulate the economy? No. You would either put a freeze on hiring (in the hopes Obamacare will be repealed or overturned by the Supreme Court), out-source jobs to other countries, or create a second company (which will grow more slowly than if you concentrated your resources) to avoid the penalty. That's where we are today, and that's why we have record unemployment. This isn't rocket science.

Obamacare also slaps companies who already insure their employees with $3,000 fines per employee if the health-care benefits they offer aren't up to Obama's standards. The White Castle hamburger chain ran the numbers and discovered that these new regulations will eat up 55 percent of their net income after 2014.[5] How in the world can anyone expect businesses to hire new workers under these kinds of insane requirements?

Not surprisingly, the instant businesses began crunching the numbers, thousands of businesses and states began asking for "waivers" from Obamacare. So far just under 1,500 waivers have been granted.[6] And guess who the big winners have been? President Obama's biggest backers who championed Obamacare! More than 50 percent of the waivers have gone to union members. And in the recent round of new waivers, 20 percent of them went to Nancy Pelosi's district.[7] You just can't make this stuff up. How is it fair to let Obama's pals off the hook and grant them waivers but force the rest of America to be stuck with Obamacare? Mr. President, you need to give all Americans a waiver!

Obamacare Passed, Premiums Skyrocketed

What's incredible is that Obamacare hasn't even kicked in yet and already it's doing tremendous damage. During the health-care debate, Obama swore that passing Obamacare would "bring down the cost of health care for families, for businesses, and for the federal government." He also said that passing his plan would "lower premiums for the typical family by $2,500 a year."[8] In September 2011, the nonprofit Kaiser Family Foundation, which tracks annual employer health insurance, released a study revealing that health insurance premiums leapt 9 percent in 2011. As Senator Orrin Hatch put it, "The president's promise that his partisan health law would lower costs was just empty rhetoric."[9]

Liberals could hardly believe it—they couldn't understand how health-care costs could have risen so much when their hero Barack Obama had promised that they wouldn't. Obama claimed his socialized medicine plan would immediately "bend the cost curve downward." He said the bill's pre-2014 requirements, such as forcing employers to cover millions of adult "children" up to twenty-six years old on their parents' health plans, would push costs down. Well, the Kaiser report found that 2.3 million adult "kids" have been added so far in the wake of Obamacare passing. And guess what happened? Under Obama, the average family's health insurance premiums have risen $2,393. That's almost the exact opposite of what the president promised. How's that for "hope and change"?[10]

As business and economics columnist Robert Samuelson concluded, "The study reminds us that runaway costs are the health system's core problem; [Obamacare] does nothing to solve it—and would actually make it worse.... If roughly 30 million or so Americans get insurance and no basic changes are made in the delivery system, then added demand will lead to higher costs, longer waiting periods, or both.... [Obamacare] was also bound to raise the costs of hiring workers by compelling employers to provide expensive coverage. That prospect can't be helping job creation."[11]

Looking back, it's incredible that anyone believed Obama and Nancy Pelosi's wild rhetoric. Remember when Pelosi promised us that passing Obamacare would magically create jobs? Her exact words were even bolder. Pelosi said, "It's about jobs. In its life, it [Obamacare] will create four million jobs—400,000 jobs almost immediately."[12] *400,000 jobs almost immediately*...incredible, isn't it? Liberals were fools to have believed such garbage, especially when there were so many small business owners pleading with the government not to crush their ability to create jobs.

Obamacare Is Killing Jobs

Instead of creating new jobs, Obamacare is destroying jobs. And the worst part is yet to come, since the truly painful provisions don't kick in until 2014. Businesses like Boeing, Caterpillar, and Deere & Company are already tallying up the job-killing costs of Obamacare. The numbers are ugly. These companies will now have to find $150 million, $100 million, and $150 million respectively—and that's just the cost to meet *one provision* in the new law.[13] Where does Obama think these sums will come from? Does he not understand that businesses exist to make a profit? Every time government adds a cost to a business, that company either has to pass the cost along to consumers, fire or stop hiring workers, or both. These three companies are big enough to absorb Obamacare's body blow and still survive. But what about small businesses that are struggling to grow and would love to hire more workers? Those are the companies that will suffer the most under Obamacare. And don't forget, small businesses are our biggest jobs creators. In fact, over the last fifteen years, small businesses have been responsible for 64 percent of net new jobs.[14]

How many jobs will Obamacare kill? A study from the National Federation of Independent Business found that Obamacare could mean the loss of 1.6 million jobs, 66 percent of which would be from small businesses.[15] Obama will probably dismiss that study because it comes from an organization that has the word "business" in its name. Fine. Then maybe he should listen to the director of the nonpartisan Congressional Budget Office, who said during congressional testimony that the bill would kill 800,000 full-time jobs in the first decade alone.[16] Bottom line: as Minnesota Congressman John Kline put it, "To suggest [Obamacare] doesn't undermine job creation is to deny reality."[17]

Obamacare Will Destroy Patient Choice and Explode Spending

In addition to killing jobs, Obamacare also destroys a patient's right to choose the insurance and doctor he wants. Whole books have been written about what's wrong with Obamacare and how we can improve health care without wrecking our economy, like *The Truth about Obamacare* by Pacific Research Institute President Sally C. Pipes. But even a casual observer can see that Obama's rhetoric doesn't align with reality. Remember when Obama promised us that "if you've got health insurance, you like your doctors, you like your plan, you can keep your doctor, you can keep your plan. Nobody is talking about taking that away from you"?[18] Yeah, well that was a flat out lie. Here's why: once the law goes into full effect in 2014, one out of three employers plan to drop employee health benefits entirely and just pay the government penalty.[19] That means those workers will be shoved into the government's subsidized insurance exchanges. And nothing will make liberals happier.

As liberals see it, pushing businesses to dump their current health-care plans and funnel their workers into the government-run health-care plans is a backdoor way to drag America closer to a so-called "single payer system," otherwise known as total government-run health care. As Howard Dean joyfully said, "Most small businesses are not going to be in the health insurance business anymore after this thing goes into effect."[20] So the line Obama sold the country about everyone being able to keep the plan they have was a total con job. As the president knew all along, millions of workers' current insurance plans will be scrapped entirely. Obamacare is nothing more than a lurch toward total government-controlled health care.

It's crazy that this plan was even proposed—America is a debtor nation. How in the world does it make sense to create a budget-busting government program like Obamacare when the United States is already $15 trillion in the hole? It's financial suicide.

The original price tag Obama and his liberal supporters quoted us was also a total sham. Not wanting to quote a price that used the word "trillion," Obama and Pelosi made sure to jigger the numbers so that he could claim Obamacare would cost $940 billion over the decade. Yet as Dr. Jeffrey H. Anderson points out, "Even this colossal tally is like the introductory price quoted by a cell phone provider. It's the price before you pay for minutes, fees, and overcharges—and before the price balloons after the introductory offer expires." Using the CBO's numbers, Anderson calculates that Obamacare's actual cost from 2014 (when the plan fully kicks in) to 2023 will be $2.0 trillion, more than double what Obama and Pelosi claimed, in order to insure the 30 million Americans Obama says are uninsured.[21] As usual, liberals play a shell game with how much they're planning to screw taxpayers for. The Obama administration said they would pay for the program by slashing $575 billion from Medicare and make up the rest in tax hikes. I think we can count on tax hikes—lots of them.

Now take a closer look at that number of uninsured Americans—30 million. Throughout the health-care debate, Obama chronically talked about the "46 million uninsured Americans." Over and over we had that number pounded into us like a nail. Then, all of a sudden, Obama decided that, no, the actual number of people who couldn't get health-care coverage was 30 million. That's quite a drop! But of course he used the smaller number after having blasted the inflated number far and wide.

But pretend for a moment that the 46 million was real. According to the ultra right-wing *New York Times*, here's how that number breaks down "with the caveat that there is overlap in these numbers" (which is why they don't exactly add up to 46 million). One out of five of the people he claimed were uninsured weren't even U.S. citizens! Another 13.7 million have plenty of money to buy health care (they make more than $75,000 a year) but choose not to get it. Eleven million poorer Americans are Medicaid or SCHIP eligible but just haven't enrolled yet. That leaves 13 million young people (ages nineteen to twenty-nine) who are either fresh out of college, can afford insurance but think they're invincible, are in-between jobs, or who are searching for jobs. [22] There's no doubt some of these folks need a safety net under them until they start their careers. The question is, was it worth it to jeopardize the world's greatest health-care system and shackle America with $2 trillion of additional debt to address the temporary health-care needs of 4 percent of the country? Or could we have devised a smarter, more efficient, less expensive solution that would have accomplished the same goal? Only a fool would choose the former over the latter.

We may get lucky and have the Supreme Court declare Obamacare unconstitutional. After all, there's no doubt that the government forcing all citizens to buy a product is a direct violation of the Commerce Clause. That would set a very dangerous precedent. "If Congress may require that individuals purchase a particular good or service," says Utah Senator Orrin Hatch, "we could simply require that Americans buy certain cars.... For that matter, we could attack the obesity problem by requiring Americans to buy fruits and vegetables."[23] Hatch is right. The individual mandate is a massive federal overreach and is clearly unconstitutional. But as every conservative knows, the Supreme Court tramples on the Constitution all the time. So it's anyone's guess what they will do.

Still, I think we've got an even chance that the Supreme Court may strike down Obamacare's so-called "individual mandate" to buy health insurance. If that happens, even Obama's supporters concede it will all but kill Obamacare, because the whole thing hinges on the government forcing everyone to buy insurance whether they want to or not. But it's anyone's guess if the Supreme Court will rule properly.

Bring Down Costs through Competition

Regardless of what happens in the Supreme Court, and even if we elect a real president who will get tough and repeal Obamacare, we still need a plan to bring down health-care costs and make health-care insurance more affordable for everyone. It starts with increasing competition between insurance companies. Competition makes everything better and more affordable. When I build a building, I let various builders and architects compete for the contract. Why? Because it sharpens their game, makes them bid competitively on price, and encourages them to give me the best quality product possible. That's true for any service or product. That's why Americans need more options when it comes to purchasing health-care insurance.

One way to infuse more competition into the market is to let citizens purchase health-care plans across state lines. Health-care costs vary drastically from state to state. For example, a 25-year-old in California can buy an HMO plan that costs him $260 a month. But for a New Yorker to buy a similar plan with equivalent benefits, it will cost him $1,228 a month.[24] Why not allow people to buy health insurance across state lines and make companies compete to offer the best plans at the best rates?

This could be easily accomplished if Congress got some guts and did the right thing. The U.S. Constitution gives Congress control over interstate commerce. But for whatever reason, the Congress has never exercised this power regarding health insurance. Bills for interstate insurance compacts have been proposed for over six years. As usual, though, the politicians in Washington have done nothing about it. They need to. As former Florida

Congressman Thomas Feeney points out, creating a national market for health-care plans would help bring costs down for lower-income Americans—such as those 19- to 29-year-olds without coverage—and give them more affordable options.[25]

The reason prices vary so much from state to state is because states differ wildly on the kinds of mandates they require in their coverage plans. As Devon Herrick, a senior fellow with the National Center for Policy Analysis, puts it: "If consumers do not want expensive 'Cadillac' health plans that pay for acupuncture, fertility treatments or hairpieces, they could buy from insurers in a state that does not mandate such benefits."[26] Increasing competition is common sense. We need to pass laws that encourage it.

Real Tort Reform Right Now

The other way we can drive down costs is by recognizing that doctors today are practicing "defensive medicine." In other words, doctors often order unnecessary tests and procedures to avoid being sued. Pricewaterhouse Coopers did a study to see how much defensive medicine adds to overall medical costs. They found that this phenomenon accounts for at least 10 percent of all medical costs.[27] That's huge.

It's not hard to understand why doctors engage in defensive medicine. Just look at disgraced Democratic vice presidential nominee John Edwards. In his former life, Edwards was a world-class ambulance chaser. In just twelve years, Edwards won $175 million in malpractice judgments by suing doctors, insurance companies, and hospitals for causing infant cerebral palsy. And this despite the fact that the American College of Obstetricians and Gynecologists has stated that the "vast majority" of cerebral palsy cases have nothing to do with the way a baby is delivered.[28] It's just one more example of what a disgraceful human being John Edwards is.

"The courts are clogged up with these cases," says Dr. Cecil Wilson of the American Medical Association. "Physicians are afraid of being hauled into court and as a result order tests they ordinarily would not order."[29] With sleazy characters like Edwards lurking around every hospital corner, it's no wonder doctors feel forced to add all those expensive tests to protect themselves. Doing so, however, jacks up our health-care costs by at least 10 percent. That's why we need serious tort reform. Specifically, we need to cap damages for so-called "pain and suffering" at $100,000. We also need "loser pays" laws that make the loser pay the legal bills of the winner if the charges are deemed baseless—a system followed by almost all other western democracies. This will help cut down on frivolous suits that artificially raise health-care costs and clog up our courts. The state of Texas recently passed loser pays legislation. Other states should do the same.

⋙·⋘

There's a reason most Americans oppose Obamacare: it's a total disaster. Barack Obama has put us so deep in the debt hole that America can't afford another one of his $2 trillion spending programs. Obamacare is already making health-care costs rise, and the thing hasn't even gone into full effect yet. Worse, it's absolutely slaughtering jobs. No businessperson with a brain would consider serious expansion with this regulatory nightmare hanging over them. Whether through a Supreme Court ruling or a presidential election, America must repeal Obamacare once and for all.

Destroying the world's finest health-care system so that Obama can have his socialized medicine program is reckless and foolish. The proper way to bring the cost of health-care down is to make insurance companies compete nationally and get defensive medicine under control through serious tort reform that includes loser pays provisions.

We need a president who will get tough and repeal Obamacare on day one. When they do, they will have accomplished more with one stroke of the pen than Obama has accomplished in his abysmal presidency. 2012 can't come soon enough.

NINE

IT'S CALLED ILLEGAL IMMIGRATION FOR A REASON

We've been inundated with criminal activity.
It's just—it's been outrageous.[1]

—**Arizona Governor Jan Brewer**

Illegal immigration is a wrecking ball aimed at U.S. taxpayers. Washington needs to get tough and fight for "We the People," not for the special interests who want cheap labor and a minority voting bloc. Every year taxpayers are getting stuck with a $113 billion bill to pay for the costs of illegal immigration.[2] That's a bill we can't afford and wouldn't have to pay if people in Washington did their jobs and upheld our nation's laws.

Too many Republicans in Washington turn a blind eye to illegal immigration because some of their business supporters want artificially cheap labor. Liberal Democrats, on the other hand, look on illegal immigrants as another potential Democrat voting bloc eager for their big government agenda of welfare handouts, class warfare, and "affirmative action." What do taxpayers get? They get the shaft.

Illegal Criminals Have Got to Go

Both sides need to grow up and put America's interests first—and that means doing what's right for our economy, our national security, and our public safety. According to a Government Accountability Office (GAO) 2011 report, America's prisons house 351,000 criminal aliens who committed a crime *after* having already broken the law by entering America illegally. Making taxpayers pay for 351,000 criminals who should never have been here in the first place is ridiculous. The GAO says that the annual price tag to incarcerate these thugs is $1.1 billion. And get this: criminal aliens have an *average* of seven arrests.[3] That's at least seven crimes committed against American citizens by each of these criminals who should never have been allowed across our borders.

According to the *New York Times*, one out of every three federal prison inmates is a Latino, and three quarters of these are here illegally.[4] As one Phoenix, Arizona, assistant federal defender put it, "I have Anglo and Native American clients who tell me about being the only non-Spanish speaker in their pod. Ten years ago, it just wasn't that way. . . . A lot of times the guards don't speak the language. How do you safely guard people who may not understand your orders?"[5] A better question is why should we have to guard them at all? Have we suddenly become an annex of Mexico's prison system? If so, Mexico should pay for it. I actually have a theory that Mexico is sending their absolute worst, possibly including prisoners, in order for us to bear the cost, both financial and social. This would account for the fact that there is so much crime and violence.

We shouldn't want lawbreakers as citizens—and that's what illegal immigrants are by definition: lawbreakers. Yes, America is a nation of immigrants, but that doesn't mean we have to offer citizenship to everyone who crosses our borders. I'd guess just about every poor person in the world wants to come here. Who wouldn't want to come to the greatest nation on earth? But that obviously is crazy. What is not crazy is having an immigration policy where we decide which potential immigrants are entitled to citizenship, where we choose the best and most productive people who want to come here for that honor. We should not let ourselves become the dumping ground for other countries' undesirables. Instead we should roll out a welcome mat only to those who can make our country better—and illegal immigrant criminals don't do that.

The illegal immigrant crime problem is far more serious and threatening than most people understand. Along our southern border, our citizens, police, and border patrol agents are being attacked with increasing brutality and regularity. Did you know that three border patrol agents are assaulted every day along America's southern border? And it's getting worse. According to the Justice Department, assaults against U.S. border patrol agents have spiked 46 percent.[6]

Then there is the "most dangerous gang in the world," the Mara Salvatrucha, more commonly known as the MS-13 gang. The gang, comprised mostly of Central American immigrants, is known for its extreme viciousness. Besides smuggling (and abusing) illegal immigrants into the United States, MS-13 might be conspiring with terrorists. Al Qaeda is always looking for a way to smuggle terrorists into our country, and American officials know that a top al Qaeda lieutenant (who had also been in Canada seeking nuclear material for a so-called "dirty bomb") met with leaders of MS-13 about ways to infiltrate America through our border with Mexico.[7] Intelligence agencies have also spotted several known members of the Somalia-based Al Shabaab Islamic terror group in Mexico and have warned that they are planning to penetrate the United States.[8]

MS-13 represents a lethal threat to both our citizens and illegal immigrants. The gang brags that they are "immigrant hunters." They lie in wait at immigration checkpoints knowing that illegals will jump off trains. MS-13 then holds the stranded illegal aliens for ransom. With 22,000 illegal immigrant kidnappings occurring each year, it's estimated that gangs like MS-13 could be raking in upwards of $50 million annually.[9]

Obviously not all illegal immigrants are members of violent gangs. Many aliens are just seeking a better life for their families. Who could fault them? But again, we cannot become a repository for all the poor and desperate people of the world. For America to change its culture and way of life, to give away American jobs at a time of high unemployment to non-citizens who have broken the law to come here, is to commit economic and cultural suicide.

And not enforcing our laws leads directly to the deaths of American citizens. Here is a poignant example. In 2010, Carlos Montano, an illegal immigrant, killed a 66-year-old nun, Sister Denise Mosier, and critically injured two others when Montano was driving drunk in a Virginia suburb. Incredibly, Carlos Montano had been arrested not once but twice before on drunk-driving charges and had other traffic-related arrests. But when

Montano got handed off to Immigration and Customs Enforcement (ICE) for deportation, the Department of Homeland Security inexplicably let Montano walk. "We handed him over to the feds assuming he would be deported," said Corey Steward, chairman of the Prince William County's Board of Supervisors. "But instead federal authorities released him back into the neighborhood and he killed a nun.... Blood is on the hands of Congress for not properly funding immigration enforcement."[10]

The needless death of Sister Denise Mosier is hardly an isolated case. There are countless stories of driving fatalities and serious injuries by people who should not have been on American roads in the first place. When liberals like Barack Obama hear tragic stories like that of Sister Mosier, they come back with, "Yes, and that's precisely why we should grant 'undocumented workers'"—that's illegals to you and me—"driver's licenses and teach them the rules of our roads!" It's a level of cluelessness that borders on delusion.

Look, my wife is an immigrant—a *legal* immigrant. Did she have to jump through legal hoops? Of course. Did she complain about it? No, she didn't. She is grateful for the chance to live in America. So she complied with the laws of the land. She worked hard to become a U.S. citizen—and the U.S. got a good one.

Illegals Are Breaking Our Bank

In purely economic terms, however, one of illegal immigration's biggest costs to taxpayers involves the monies paid to educate the children of illegal aliens. Illegal immigrant children often require special classes and language specialists, and take time and resources away from our own students. On this point I strongly disagree with Governor Rick Perry. The Federation for American Immigration Reform (FAIR) reports that U.S. taxpayers shell out $52 billion annually to educate illegal aliens. Liberals like to say that illegal aliens pay taxes too in the form of sales taxes and the fees and taxes that get folded into the costs of things like gasoline. But this argument fails—big time. According to FAIR, on average, less than 5 percent of the public costs associated with illegals are regained through taxes paid by illegal aliens.[11]

The fact is when it comes to taxpayer-provided social services and welfare, illegal aliens have elbowed their way to the front of the line. In 2011, the *Houston Chronicle* reported that *70 percent* of the illegal immigrant families living in Texas received welfare assistance. That's compared to the already too high 39 percent of native-born Americans who receive welfare.[12] That's insane. People who broke into the country use our social safety net with greater regularity than our own citizens! How can we ever expect to get a handle on the illegal immigration crisis when we incentivize and reward it with free welfare checks and health care?

"We can no longer afford to be HMO to the world," says Los Angeles County Supervisor Michael Antonovich. He says that the total cost to taxpayers for illegal immigrants in Los Angeles County is $1.6 billion, "not including the hundreds of millions of dollars for education."[13]

The root cause of all the welfare payments to illegal aliens is the so-called "anchor baby" phenomenon, which is when illegal immigrant mothers have a baby on American soil. The child automatically becomes an American citizen, though this was *never* the intention of the Fourteenth Amendment, which states, "All citizens born or naturalized in the United States, and subject to the jurisdiction thereof, are citizens of the United States and the state wherein they reside." The clear purpose of the Fourteenth Amendment, ratified in 1868, three years after the end of the Civil War, was to guarantee full citizenship rights to now emancipated former slaves. It was not intended to guarantee untrammeled immigration to the United States.

Some 4 million anchor babies are now officially U.S. citizens. This has to stop. The only other major country in the world that issues citizenship based on where one's mother delivers her child is Canada. The rest of the world bases citizenship on who the kid's parents are, which is of course the only sane standard.[14] If a pregnant American mother is traveling to Egypt on business and goes into delivery, do we instantly declare her child an Egyptian? Of course not. But that's precisely what goes on every day in America: women who have zero connection to the United States cross the border, deliver a baby, and their kid magically becomes an American citizen eligible to receive all the rights and benefits of those who have lived, worked, and paid taxes in our country.

Republican Senators John Kyl of Arizona and Lindsey Graham of South Carolina have discussed introducing a constitutional amendment to clarify and restore the original intent of the Fourteenth Amendment. It's long past time that America joins the rest of the world in granting citizenship along rational lines.

Liberal Myths

But in restoring sanity to the interpretation and enforcement of our laws, we'll have to fight liberal myths every step of the way. We've all heard a million times: "We need illegal immigrants because they are willing to do jobs Americans just won't." To that one I say, "Says who?" We have 25 million citizens who need jobs, and 7 million illegal immigrants holding American jobs. Do the math. If illegal aliens weren't holding these jobs, American citizens would, because these jobs need to be filled, and guess what? Those jobs would pay more than they do now, because illegal low-wage workers drive down wage rates. Even the *Washington Post* has conceded that "an influx of immigrants has helped depress the incomes of low-skilled workers in recent decades, many economists agree."[15] As research by Harvard University economist George J. Borjas has shown, "the primary losers in this country are workers who do not have high school diplomas, particularly blacks and native-born Hispanics." Borjas found that from 1980 to 2000, illegal immigrants lowered the nation's average wages some 7.4 percent for America's 10 million native-born men who lack a high school diploma.[16] You would think that Obama, who talks a good game about caring for the poor, would try to help raise wages for people at the bottom of the economic ladder. But with black teenage unemployment now at a staggering 46.5 percent, and with the overall black underemployment rate at a breathtaking 18.8 percent, it's outrageous that the president continues to mock Republican efforts to reduce illegal immigration and boost wages.[17]

"All the stuff they [Republicans] ask for, we've done," said Obama at a 2011 immigration rally in El Paso, Texas. "Maybe they'll need a moat," Obama said to laughter. "Maybe they want alligators in the moat! They'll never be satisfied."[18]

Mr. President, you might think the border deaths, narco terrorists, and waves of violent illegal criminals into America are a joke, but the people who live along the border and the communities under siege do not. We need a president who will get tough, enforce our laws, protect our people, and pull wages up.

One of the biggest myths we have been told is that illegal immigrants actually produce a net gain economically. This is a cute argument, but it's a complete joke. It assumes, among other things, that illegal workers keep their money here in America. But they don't. In 2006, 73 percent of Latino immigrants regularly sent money back to their home countries, amounting to $45 billion. For countries like Mexico, illegal immigrants in the United States are a cash cow. In fact, Mexico's second biggest source of foreign income, just behind oil exports, comes from—you guessed it—remittances from illegal aliens. In 2008, Mexico got $25.1 billion in money sent back home. Remittances have skyrocketed over the last decade. They went from $9 billion in 2001 to $26 billion in 2007.[19] That's money that American workers could be earning, saving, and spending here in the United States.

So what to do?

Reform Our Illegal Immigration System

Before I lay out what needs to be done to get our illegal immigration mess fixed, it's worth first discussing what America needs to do with our *legal* immigration system. It, too, is backwards and in need of a total overhaul. Thankfully, our neighbors to the north, Canada, have a smart, merit-based plan that America should adopt.

Canada's legal immigration plan starts with a simple and smart question: How will any immigrant applying for citizenship "support the development of a strong, prosperous Canadian economy"? Economic benefit should be our chief aim. America doesn't need freeloaders who come here to live off our welfare system. We need legal immigrants who bring skills, prosperity, and intellectual capital. In Canada, aliens applying for permanent residence are awarded points based on their skills and how they will benefit the Canadian economy. Only 40 percent of the overall determination on whether permanent residence will be granted depends on family relationships or refugee status. The remaining 60 percent of the decision hinges on how the immigrant will add value to Canada's economy. Our system is almost exactly the opposite. In fact, it's worse. Seventy percent of the one million permanent resident admissions the United States grants every year are based on family relations. Only 13 percent depend on employment (the remainder are for refugees and diversity visas).[20] This makes no sense whatsoever.

For a Canadian applicant to be considered for permanent residency, he must score a minimum of 67 points out of 100. He must also have a minimum of one year of full-time work experience in a desired skill area within the last ten years. The better the immigrant's attributes, the higher the score. If the alien doesn't earn 67 points and is serious about wanting to live in Canada, he can work on developing his marketable skills until he does qualify. For example, if the applicant isn't a college graduate, he can go home, get a college degree, and add 25 points to his total and reapply. As a result, roughly half of Canada's immigrants have a bachelor's degree.[21]

Canada's legal immigration system also requires that before an immigrant qualifies for Canada's equivalent of Social Security, he has to have been resident in the country for at least ten of his adult years. In America, we only require five years.[22]

Work Visas

Our country's leaders are just so plain stupid. As an example, foreign students come over to our colleges, learn everything there is to learn about physics, finance, mathematics, and computers, and graduate with honors. They would love to stay in this country, but we don't allow them to. We immediately ship them back to their country to use all of the knowledge they learned at the best colleges in the United States back in their country rather than keep it here in ours.

When we have gifted people in this country we should cherish them and let them stay. But instead we fling our arms wide open to the lowlifes, the criminals, the people who have no intention to contribute to our country. We spend billions of dollars taking care of them as they, in many cases, run rampant through our streets, doing many things you're not supposed to do. But the great ones, we immediately expel.

Wouldn't it be better if we invited foreign students graduating from our colleges to stay to build American companies, instead of foreign companies that will be wreaking havoc against Boeing, Caterpillar, and many other of our great American companies in the future?

If we adopted this commonsense merit-based approach, our immigration policy would be guided by what benefits America. That's the way it ought to be. If American businesses need immigrants with particular technical skills, by all means, let's hire them. The privilege of becoming an American citizen should be about the value an immigrant brings to our country, not about an open door for anyone and everyone who wants to come here.

Bottom line: living in America is the greatest blessing a person could ever receive. If people want to live and work here, they should bring something to the table, not just be feasting off it.

The 5-Point Trump Plan

Now, as for what to do about illegal immigration, we should follow the repeal of the anchor baby provisions with a five-point program to create a smart and humane plan to get illegal immigration under control. It starts with securing our borders. Look, if a nation can't protect its own borders, it ceases to be a country. We're not just some landmass that anyone who wants to can trample on at will. I believe America is an exceptional nation worthy of protection. That requires getting tough on border enforcement. We can and should have a robust debate over whether that means continuing to build the physical border fence or utilizing "virtual fences" that use lasers as trip wires to monitor illegal border crossings.

From the research my people have shown me, I'm not impressed with the mediocre success rates of the current crop of virtual fences that have been developed and tested. I am, however, impressed with the success of the double- and triple-layered fence in places like Yuma, Arizona. The wall there is a serious 20-foot wall. It has three walls separated by 75-yard "no man's lands" for border agents to zoom up and down in vehicles. It also has cameras, radio systems, radar, and pole-topped lights.[23] "This wall works," says U.S. border patrol agent Michael Bernacke. "A lot of people have the misconception that it is a waste of time and money, but the numbers of apprehensions show that it works." After the triple-layered fence was installed, the 120-mile stretch of the U.S.-Mexican border known as the Yuma sector experienced a 72 percent plunge in illegal immigrant apprehensions. Before the fence was installed, 800 people were apprehended attempting to enter America each day. Post-fence, that number was 50 or fewer.[24]

Some say Yuma's flat terrain makes it a special case and that other parts of the border aren't conducive to that kind of fence. In that case, we just need to be ready to build other kinds of fences, too. The point is that properly built walls work. We just need the political will to finish the job. And by the way, finishing the job will employ a lot of construction workers. Moreover, I call on Congress and the president to hire another 25,000 border patrol agents and give them the aerial equipment they need, such as Predator drones, to provide real-time aerial reconnaissance information to agents guarding the border wall.

Second, we need a president who will enforce our laws. Right now, in a sneaky attempt to appease the strong and well-organized pro-amnesty lobby, the Department of Homeland Security has, on Obama's orders, put a freeze on the deportation of 300,000 illegal immigrants.

The administration says it wants to review each case individually and will only deport illegal aliens with criminal records, and that "no enforcement resources will be expended on those who do not pose a threat to public safety."[25]

This wholesale abdication of a president's constitutional duties is as shocking as it is foolish. It's political pandering of the worst kind. Worse, Obama has said these aliens who were slated for deportation can obtain work permits![26] So in Obama we have a president who is not only not enforcing our laws, he is helping illegal immigrants to break them further! Obama wants to *reward* illegal immigrants by giving them the chance to take yet another American job. "The lesson for illegal aliens," says James R. Edwards Jr., coauthor of *The Congressional Politics of Immigration Reform*, is that if they get "caught, they can escape immigration trouble, win legal status and seek a work permit."[27]

How can we ask our brave U.S. border agents to risk their lives when the commander in chief is just going to shrug his shoulders and let 300,000 illegals make a mockery of our laws? It's a total disgrace. Obama should be ashamed to play politics on an issue of such national importance. But he's not. He thinks it's cute and makes jokes about it, and he thinks it will win him votes on the insulting assumption that Latino Americans don't care about America's laws. The evidence is clear that President Obama certainly doesn't care about America's immigration laws. After all, two of his relatives—his uncle Omar Onyango Obama (arrested for drunk driving in Massachusetts) and his aunt Zeituni Onyango—are illegal aliens who have magically avoided deportation, with his aunt having finally been awarded asylum. Republican Congressman Steve King of Iowa has called for congressional hearings into whether the White House intervened on behalf of President Obama's relatives. But of course the bigger scandal is that it is Obama administration policy to give special treatment to all illegal aliens—to treat them as if they are legal.

You just can't make this stuff up. Can you imagine the national firestorm the liberal media would have stoked had President George W. Bush had not one but *two* illegal immigrant family members who had received special treatment and been permitted to stay in America?[28] Or what if President Bush had failed to enforce environmental laws and gave orders to federal agencies to help businesses break such laws? Democrats would have called for Bush's impeachment. But not this president. The liberal media protect Obama every way they can.

The third thing we need to do is overturn Obama's insane new ICE recommendations for illegal immigrant detention facilities. In an effort to coddle illegal aliens, officials at nine detention facilities have now been instructed to make the following changes:

- Soften the look for the facility with hanging plants, flower baskets, new paint colors…wall graphics and framed pictures on the walls, and enhance the aesthetics of the living areas.…
- Expand programming for detainees to include movie nights, bingo, arts and crafts, dance, walk and exercise classes, health and welfare classes, basic cooking classes, tutoring and self-paced computer training on portable computer stations.…

- Provide celebrations of special occasions and [allow] a detainee to receive outside, packaged food for celebrations....

- Provide fresh carrot sticks and celery or other vegetables in a bar format....

- Provide self-serve beverage bars....

- Offer water and tea in the housing area at all times.

- Provide a unit manager so detainees have someone available to talk to and to solve problems in the facility other than the immediate guard....

- Survey community-based immigration advocacy groups and immigration attorneys for suggestions that may improve communication and ease of access....

- Increase availability of legal supplies and postage...for legal correspondence.

- Add research resources at the law libraries....

- [Provide] non-penal clothing for detainees to wear.

- Eliminate lock downs and lights out....

- Reduce the frequency of and...wholly eliminate pat down searches....

- Provide four hours or more hours of recreation in a natural setting....

- Provide internet-based free phone service.

- Provide email access for detainees....[29]

That's right, your government now requires resort-like accommodations—paid for by you, the American taxpayer—to reward the flood of people entering our country illegally. Obama has turned America into a laughingstock. Our next president must stop this insanity.

The next part of my plan involves opposing the so-called DREAM Act, which grants in-state tuition benefits at public colleges and universities to illegal immigrant college students. The Development, Relief, and Education for Alien Minors (DREAM) proposal is yet another attempt by Obama and his pro-amnesty pals to create new anchors and rewards for those who defy our laws.

So get this: under the DREAM Act, if you're not a citizen but a child of illegal immigrants, then you get in-state tuition benefits, but if you're a legal citizen living out of state, you have to pay higher tuition. So an American student in Texas who wants to go to college in Arizona will have to pay more in tuition than a non-citizen student living illegally in Arizona. How fair is that? The fact that legislation like the DREAM Act has even seen the light of day shows you just how upside down our immigration policies have become—and just how far politicians are willing to pander to what they see as a Latino voting bloc. Sacrificing American laws on the altar of political expediency is immoral. If Congress is ever foolish enough to pass legislation that grants tuition breaks for illegal aliens, America's next president must have the political courage and constitutional conviction to veto it.

⇥⋅⇤

Democrats need to respect our laws, respect the fact that Latino Americans are as interested in the rule of law as anyone else, respect the immigrants who are patiently and lawfully standing in line for legal citizenship, and most of all respect our own citizens who should not have the rule of law, their jobs, even their lives and their nation's future put at risk by irresponsible Washington politicians. That's the sort of "hope and change" we need, not a commander in chief who thinks border security and the rule of law is a joke.

TEN

THE AMERICA
OUR CHILDREN DESERVE

*Freedom is never more than one generation away
from extinction. We didn't pass it to our children in
the bloodstream. It must be fought for, protected,
and handed on for them to do the same.*

—President Ronald Reagan

Barack Obama has done an incredible job of tarnishing our kids' futures.

He's saddled our children with more debt than we accumulated in 225 years in America. He's bowed down to China and allowed them to steal our economic future through currency manipulation and ripping off our technological and military secrets. He's failed to stand up to the Middle Eastern oil mobsters known as OPEC who think they can hold us hostage through higher prices at the pump. He's unleashed Obamacare on our small businesses and brought job creation and hiring to a screeching halt.

And he's created an economic climate where young people out of college face incredible uncertainty. Three years ago, 90 percent of college graduates landed a job out of college. Today, under the community organizer, that figure is a depressing 56 percent.[1]

I love America. I'm saddened by what I see happening to our country. We're being humiliated, disrespected, and badly abused. Obama was a leftist experiment that has failed and gone horribly wrong, and everyone knows it. Even friends of mine who voted for the guy privately admit that he's been a huge disappointment. We cannot afford four more years of this mess. Our children's futures are on the line—and we have to come through for them. We have to get tough so that our country can be great again.

We have to get tough on OPEC. These oil thugs rip us off year after year. We've had no leadership in Washington willing to stand up to them and put a stop to it. We have spent hundreds of billions of dollars and thousands of lives in Iraq, and now Libya, and gotten nothing in return but disrespect and ingratitude. That must end. Now. I say we take the oil. No more free military support. Either you pay us to defend you or we take the oil. It's fair and smart, which is probably why the politicians in Washington haven't implemented it.

We have to get tough on China. For every one American child there are four Chinese. China is out to steal our kids' jobs, and so far they're doing a tremendous job of it. They've manipulated their currency to such an unbelievable degree that they have destroyed our manufacturing sector. It's time to bring American manufacturing back to life. It's encouraging that the U.S. finally did as I have been saying for over a year and got tough on China's currency manipulation. The president should sign that measure into law effective immediately. Unfair trade is not free trade. China cheats and wins to the tune of more than $300 billion a year. No more. They either must play by the rules or they pay the price. End of story.

It's time our leaders in Washington wake up and realize that China's massive military buildup is producing weapons with our names on them. Our kids are the ones who will be facing down the Chinese in the years to come. If we don't get tough and put a stop to their rampant theft of our military and technological secrets, we will have failed the next generation of Americans miserably. Those who pretend China is our friend are either naïve, incompetent, or both. The Chinese can be reined in easily—we are their biggest customer. All we need is a president willing to stand up, not bow down, to China.

I believe we are at a monumental fork in the American road. I always say that the next election is the "most important election" in our lifetimes. Our national debt is at $15 trillion. Just imagine what Obama will do if he knows he's not facing reelection? What kind of damage to our national security and international standing will we suffer over the next four years with Obama bowing down to a rising Russia and China? It's horrifying to think about.

America the Exceptional

But maybe my biggest beef with Obama is his view that there's nothing special or exceptional about America—that we're no different than any other country. If a guy is that clueless about the character of America, he has no business being the leader of America. Our country is the greatest force for freedom the world has ever known. We have big hearts, big brains, and big guts—and we use all three. In the past our free market capitalist system has created more wealth and prosperity than any government-controlled economy could ever dream of doing. Because of that wealth, we give more in charity than any other country, and twice as much as the second most generous nation.[2]

Obama thinks America would be better off if we acted more like European socialist countries—many of which are in default and economic freefall. I think America would be better off if we ditch the community organizer experiment and get back to being the America we've been since our Founding Fathers risked their lives to create our country.

In 2012, our nation needs to send Barack Obama a message. We need to say loud and clear: Mr. President, we're not interested in your utopian vision of "fundamentally transforming America." We like the vision our Founding Fathers and the Constitution created just fine. If that's what you meant by "hope and change," you can keep the change. We're not interested.

We need a leader who will get tough, get smart, and get America working again. I believe America is worth fighting for. I believe America has nothing to apologize for. I believe America can get back her greatness. But we need a tough leader for tough times—someone who isn't afraid to do hard things. We must find and elect that leader so our children and grandchildren will inherit an America as free and safe as the one we grew up in. The price of failure is too great—we have to succeed. The fate of freedom rests on it.

We have to get tough on the notion that government is the solution to every problem. It's not. As President Reagan said, "Government isn't the solution to our problem. Government is the problem." Barack Obama is the most liberal president the United States has ever dared to elect. When he was running for office, Obama warned the country that his goal was to "fundamentally transform America" and that he believed in "spreading the wealth around." Now, with three years under his belt, America looks like an economic wasteland. One out of every five men you pass on your way to work is out of work. Every seventh person you pass on the sidewalk is now on food stamps. Forty-six million Americans—more than at any time ever in the history of this country—now live under the poverty line. Businesses are being shuttered. Foreclosure rates are at historic highs. For the first time in American history, the United States has lost its triple-A credit rating. Gas prices have doubled. Our national debt has exploded. Jobs and economic growth are nowhere in sight.

How can we feel good about handing over this mess to our children and grandchildren? How can we think about the hundreds of thousands of soldiers, sailors, airmen, and Marines who have died for our freedom and way of life and not be ashamed at how we've allowed their gift to be trashed and abused? It's a total disgrace. If we're going to turn this thing around, we have to do it fast.

It's time to get tough. The time is now.

THE PRESS AND
THE PRESIDENCY

n the spring of 2011, Lally Weymouth, daughter of the late, great Katherine Graham, publisher of the *Washington Post*, invited me to go to the
White House Correspondents' Dinner. I had turned down so many of
Lally's invitations in the past, I thought accepting her invite would be the
right thing to do. I knew I was probably being set up by the media, but
that's okay as long as you're prepared for it.

When I arrived at the event in Washington, thousands of people were
packed into DC's biggest ballroom. The White House Correspondents'
Dinner is the Academy Awards of politics. News reporters, political opera-
tives, celebrities—you name it they're all there. As I walked in, the paparazzi

and press were going crazy. "Mr. Trump, Mr. Trump," they shouted, "do you think the president will mention you in his speech?" I said, "I have absolutely no idea. I never thought about it, I sincerely doubt it, and why would he mention me?" I said this honestly despite the fact that I was at the top of the polls without even campaigning. The truth is, if I was in Obama's position, I probably wouldn't have mentioned the name Donald Trump, especially since I was hitting him hard on his birth certificate and asking why he wouldn't just show it and get on with dealing with the serious issues our country faces today on debt, unemployment, and China, among others.

In any event, the festivities started, people went to the dais and made speeches, and eventually a third-rate comedian named Seth Meyers (somebody who in my opinion has absolutely no talent) got up and spoke. He was nervous, shaking, and sounded like he had marbles in his mouth. He made a crack that Donald Trump's candidacy was a joke or something to that effect. It was quite nasty but I've had a lot worse things said about me.

Then the president got up. As part of his routine they had a picture of the so-called birth certificate blown up on a large screen. And while the president was smiling, I knew inside he wasn't. Then, they showed a picture of the White House with "Trump White House" written on top of it like a hotel sign, which was cute. The president spent a lot of time telling jokes about me. I didn't quite know how to react. Should I be laughing? Smiling? Frowning? I wasn't sure so I decided to keep a straight face, with a few little smiles every once in a while because I knew the cameras were on me. The fact is, I loved the evening and I loved what the president was saying because even though they were jokes, he was telling them in a nice and respectful way and he did a good job telling them. And while I shouldn't admit this, I don't mind being the center of attention, especially on such an evening.

Sitting at another table was a beautiful blonde woman who turned out to be supermodel Brooklyn Decker, wife of Andy Roddick (a wonderful guy and a terrific tennis player who has never received his fair due). Brooklyn was not happy. Lally Weymouth was laughing her head off and other people were laughing like crazy. They thought it was hilarious that I was being roasted, but Brooklyn Decker actually looked angry. Months later, Brooklyn and I met at Anna Wintour's fabulous dinner at the Metropolitan Museum of Art. I thanked Brooklyn for her classy attitude and she knew exactly what I was saying. She is a terrific person and will continue to go far.

In any event, as the president was telling joke after joke, I tapped my wonderful wife, Melania, on the knee and said under my breath, "Baby, do you believe this? This is amazing. The president of the United States is doing nothing but talking about me." I loved it! I was having a great time! In fact, walking out of the ballroom, people were high-fiving me. They couldn't believe what they had just witnessed. It was a stellar night.

The next morning, I picked up the newspapers. The press was brutal. They said I was ridiculed, refused to smile, and was deeply embarrassed. I realized then and there that political life is not real life. The media can distort the truth, and everyone thinks that's what really happened. I had a great time, but the press made it seem just the opposite. So for the record, the White House Correspondents' Dinner was a real highlight for me, and I loved it immensely.

The Press

What I don't love are wannabe "journalists" who are obsessed with protecting Obama, and "reporters" who try to ride my coattails to make a name for themselves and compensate for their lack of talent. Take, for example, MSNBC. They have this guy called Lawrence O'Donnell whom

I seldom watch (and neither does anybody else). His ratings are terrible. So bad, in fact, that they just moved him from the 8:00 p.m. time slot because Bill O'Reilly was absolutely killing him.

This O'Donnell guy's hatred of me was absolutely laughable. He would rant and rave about me like a total lunatic. I don't think he has a huge career in television—at least I would be very surprised. A year ago, he had strongly picked Tim Pawlenty to win the Republican nomination. Obviously, that turned out wrong. His media bookers, who are very nice, keep calling my office begging me to do his show. Our response is simple: I only do shows that get good ratings. I don't want to waste my time.

One bright spot on MSNBC is Joe Scarborough and Mika Brzezinski on a show called *Morning Joe*. I don't always agree with what they say, but it's a vibrant, entertaining show. They have a great future in television or anything they want to do. My only suggestion for Joe and Mika is that they be more forthcoming, because often last year Mika and Joe would call me to say they were making a speech to a big audience and wanted to know if it would be okay if they could call me on my cell phone so I could say a few words during their speech. Whenever possible, I would agree to it. Mika usually would be the one to call and I would be speaking by cell phone to hundreds or thousands of people. Mika said to me, and I am sure she won't deny it, that every time they make a speech all the people ask about is Donald Trump. They want to hear about Donald Trump, they want to know what it is Donald Trump thinks. The only problem is they don't say that on the air. In fact, recently, there was a beautiful picture of Mika making a speech holding up her cell phone and Joe alluded, "Oh, look at the cell phone... I wonder what is going on there." Mika, knowing exactly what Joe was alluding to, said, "Uh, well something..." and that was the end of it and they went on to the next topic. That doesn't change my love for Joe and Mika. They are great people and they are very talented, but they should be a little bit more open about how I help them.

One guy I find somewhat irritating, but have actually come to like in terms of viewing, is Bob Beckel, the resident liberal on Fox News. I don't know the guy, but every time in the past when my name was mentioned, Beckel would say, "Well, what does he know? He went bankrupt."

When I heard this, I asked one of my people to call Fox and explain that I never went bankrupt. Over the years, I, Carl Icahn, Henry Kravis, Cerberus, Apollo, and many of the biggest names in business have used the nation's laws to do and turn great deals. I have used the laws for certain companies to reduce debt and turn them around. I have also bought companies and immediately thrown them into Chapter 11 in order to renegotiate with banks, and made great deals because of it—I followed the law, and what's wrong with that? Now, if they change the laws, I will find another way to gain maximum advantage. But the bottom line is I never went bankrupt. Anyway, I have to give credit to Beckel, because after we set him straight, he has stopped making his mistake and now I enjoy him much more.

Someone I don't enjoy is the clown called Bryant Gumbel. He has failed on so many shows I've lost count. At any rate, Gumbel goes on HBO to cover the amazing story of a golf course I am building in Scotland. Trump International Golf Links is being built on the largest dunes in the world. When completed, there won't be anything like it. In fact, I and others predict it will be the greatest golf course anywhere in the world. It's a spectacular project, but it's been controversial because some environmental groups are opposed to developing the Great Dunes of Scotland, which I happen to own. So Bryant gets on HBO to do a story on the amazing golf course and goes off on a rant about me and Obama and tries to paint me as some kind of racist, which I am the furthest thing from being. Here he gets this big story on almost 2,000 acres along the North Sea in Scotland being transformed into the world's greatest golf course, and what does he do? He launches into a temper tantrum about Donald Trump. What a jerk! About the only thing I admire about the guy is his taste in real estate—he bought a couple of apartments in one of my many buildings.

Far better than Bryant Gumbel is Piers Morgan. After winning *Celebrity Apprentice*, Piers Morgan became a star and took over for Larry King on CNN. His show is terrific. One day Piers called me and asked me whether I would call in to his show, a privilege I receive that few others get because they'd rather have me on the show by phone than not at all. So I told him I would.

It turned out that he had a guest that night who was, of all people, then-Congressman Anthony Weiner. Interestingly, this was shortly before he imploded with his death-wish antics of sending nude photos of himself to women he had never met. Think of this: a celebrity politician, well known, doing such a thing. What a loser!

About a month prior to doing the show, Anthony called me. I knew him somewhat. He asked me to support his bid for New York City mayor. I told him strongly that I liked Mike Bloomberg, who would not be running again, and that it was a little early to start thinking about it, but sure, he could come see me if he wanted to. We had a very pleasant conversation. In fact, it could not have been nicer.

So when I called in to Piers at about 9:10 p.m., I learned that Anthony was in studio and would participate in our conversation. They asked me if that was okay and I said it was fine.

Piers started off by asking me a question and then all of the sudden out of nowhere I heard this maniac Weiner ranting and raving, with great anger, about all sorts of things. He said I would never be president. I said to myself, *Wow, is this the same guy that just called me about campaign contributions?* Then I attacked him, because I always believe when attacked, hit your opponent back harder and meaner and ideally right between the eyes. Weiner said in a snide voice that he was on pace to be New York City's next mayor, whether I liked it or not. I told him that wasn't happening, at least not according to the polls and what people in the city were saying about him. He rambled for a bit and then I said, "A lot of people are leaving the city if you end up winning."

Little did I realize that a few weeks later this moron would explode, and my prediction that Anthony Weiner would not be mayor of New York City would be so prophetic and be proven correct so quickly.

As you probably know, my show *Celebrity Apprentice* has been one of NBC's biggest hit shows and a huge money maker for eleven seasons. I have a lot of rich friends who tell me they would kill to have their own hot reality show. Not for the money, mind you, but because it creates such a powerful brand presence and is a lot of fun to do. I tell them to go for it, but for whatever reason—personality, looks, stage fright, lots of reasons—they say they could never do it. But they give me a lot of credit for being able to pull it off.

Last season, *The Apprentice* was usually the #1 show in the 10:00 p.m. time slot, which is the most important time slot because it leads into the

You're hired! Bill Rancic's win propelled "The Apprentice."

TOP 25 SHOWS IN 18-49

1.	The Apprentice (NBC)	13.6/34
2.	American Idol-Wed. (Fox)	9.7/28
3.	CSI (CBS)	7.9/20
4.	Survivor (CBS)	7.6/22
4.	Friends-8:30 (NBC)	7.6/21
6.	American Idol-Thu. (Fox)	6.2/19
7.	Friends (NBC)	5.9/16
7.	Fear Factor (NBC)	5.9/17
9.	Law & Order (NBC)	5.2/14
10.	Without a Trace (CBS)	5.1/13
10.	Crossing Jordan (NBC)	5.1/13
12.	Miss USA 2004 (NBC)	4.9/12
13.	Law & Order: CI (NBC)	4.8/11
13.	The Sopranos (HBO)*	4.8/11
15.	CSI: Miami (CBS)	4.7/12
16.	The Bachelor (ABC)	4.6/12
17.	The OC (Fox)	4.4/11
18.	The Simpsons (Fox)	4.3/13
18.	Law & Order: SVU (NBC)	4.3/11
20.	That '70s Show-Tue. (Fox)	4.2/12
20.	Extreme Makeover (ABC)	4.2/11
20.	The Simpsons-8:30 (Fox)	4.2/11
23.	Dateline Special-Wed. (NBC)	4.1/10
24.	The Swan (Fox)	3.9/10
24.	Two and a Half Men-9 (CBS)	3.9/10
24.	Two and a Half Men (CBS)	3.9/9

TOP SHOWS IN 25-54

1.	The Apprentice (NBC)	14.4/32
2.	American Idol-Wed. (Fox)	10.5/28
3.	CSI (CBS)	9.8/22
4.	Survivor (CBS)	9.0/24
5.	Friends (NBC)	7.8/20

TOP CABLE NETS IN 18-49

1.	TNT	0.86
2.	USA	0.67
3.	MTV	0.61
4.	History	0.59
5.	TBS	0.57

EVENING NEWS

WEEK 30: April 12-18, 2004		
	Viewers	A25-54
ABC	9.11 million	2.4/9
CBS	7.23 million	2.0/8
NBC	10.01 million	2.7/10

Each 18-49 ratings point equals 1.28 million viewers
Each 25-54 ratings point equals 1.28 million viewers
Source: Nielsen Media Research
* not supported

local news. It's been a winner right from the beginning. Here, for instance, is a *Variety* ratings chart on its first season.

Right now we're shooting the twelfth season, which will debut right after the Super Bowl. And let me tell you, NBC is going to be happy, because we have the best cast I think we've ever had.

Nevertheless, when I announced I was thinking of running for president, some of NBC's news people absolutely smashed me. One of them was Chuck Todd. I call him "Sleepy Eyes" because he looks like he is falling asleep when he speaks. No matter what I did or how hot I was in the polls, Sleepy Eyes Chuck Todd refused to say it. I would call him and say, "Chuck, it's not fair what you're doing." He would say, "Okay, I'll change it," but he wouldn't change. The thing I find most offensive about Chuck Todd is the fact that he pretends to be an objective journalist, when in reality the guy is a partisan hack. I was very disappointed in Chuck Todd. Needless to say, he's no Tim Russert.

Look, I love NBC. They were the ones who really understood how big *The Apprentice* was going to be. ABC made an offer too, but NBC had the vision. I give Bob Wright and Jeff Zucker tremendous credit. They wouldn't let Mark Burnett or me go anywhere else. They practically locked the doors at 30 Rock until we signed.

I also think Bob Greenblatt will do a fantastic job with prime time, but they need a lot of help. Steve Burke and Brian Roberts of Comcast are going to be amazing. I already see a big difference. So I love NBC. They are very special to me and I want to see them succeed. I'm sure they will—in spite of lightweights like Lawrence O'Donnell, Sleepy Eyes Chuck Todd, and that goof Ed Schultz. I don't say that with mean-spiritedness. It's just that lackluster talent offends me. People like Matt Lauer and Jim Bell's *Today* show team are great. I hope NBC will be able to re-sign Lauer when his contract comes up so he will continue there for many years to come. I also think David Gregory is doing a fine job filling some awfully big shoes over at *Meet the Press*. David's been tough but fair—and that's all you can ask.

I do, however, think NBC made two big mistakes recently. One, they let CNN steal Erin Burnett away. I don't think Erin will be as successful on CNN, because it's very hard to do well in certain corporate cultures. Letting Erin get away was a big loss for NBC. Second, they named Brian Williams's new show *Rock Center*, a horrible name for a show—and names of shows really matter. Brian is fantastic. But *Rock Center* will never work, and if they get four or five million viewers a night it will be a lot. I hope it works out, but I think it's going to be a very long, hard road. Now, if they did it in Trump Tower and called it Trump Tower, it would, of course, be a smash hit!

One person who was very critical of me last spring but who hasn't spoken up lately is Karl Rove. I didn't know Rove, but he asked to see me quite some time ago, way before I talked about running for president. He came to my office and asked for money for his PAC. I think I gave him $100,000 or maybe more. When I was giving him money, he was a very nice guy. "There's nobody like you, Mr. Trump," he said. But then I decided—without consulting him, I guess—to consider a presidential run. I was quickly #1 in the polls, and Rove said something to the effect that mine was a clown candidacy. He already had a favorite candidate, so he felt he had to torpedo me because I was a threat. I really went after Rove. Since then, he's become nice and respectful. But I would say this: if he attacks me again I'll go after him like nobody has ever gone after him before. I didn't mind his statements about me, but I thought it was a terrible move after I gave him a six-figure donation. Life doesn't work that way—not in my world. Very stupid, very disloyal.

Plenty of media guys, like George Stephanopoulos, are big Obama fans. I like George a lot. But it was incredible to see how overprotective reporters got toward Obama when I simply said what everyone in America was thinking: "Where's the birth certificate?" I didn't actually bring up the whole birth certificate question at first—I wanted to talk about how China and OPEC are ripping us off and how we need to get tough on Iran, taxes, reckless spending, and repealing Obamacare. But when George brought it up during an interview on *Good Morning America*, he literally sprang out of his chair and started screaming at me for even questioning Obama. It was amazing. If the president were a Republican, the press wouldn't be so protective. But Obama? He must be guarded and treated with kid gloves.

I never understood why Obama would allow the question to hang around. Why not just produce the birth certificate and be done with it? Get it out there and move on. So I was very proud that I was able to finally get him to do something that no one else had been able to do. For the record, I'm not saying Obama wasn't born in the United States. However, multiple questions still surround the hospital records, his grandmother's statement that he was born out of the country, and his family members' statements that they weren't sure which hospital he was born in. As for the birth certificate I got him to produce, some people have questioned whether it's authentic. Maybe it is, maybe it isn't. That's for experts to determine. But if Obama's liberal media pals don't like my answer, stop asking the question.

Nothing irritates me more than a double standard, and yet that's what we see with liberal media types. Take Jon Stewart. I actually enjoy the guy, but when he did a segment mocking presidential candidate Herman Cain, and used a very racist and degrading tone that was insulting to the African American community, did he get booted off the air like Don Imus? No. Where was the Reverend Jesse Jackson? Where was the Reverend Al Sharpton? Where was Sleepy Eyes Chuck Todd to provide hard-hitting journalistic "analysis"? Nowhere. Stewart should have lost his job—at least temporarily. But he didn't and he won't because liberals in the media always get a free pass, no matter how bad their behavior.

Disappointing behavior by people in the press occurs on both sides of the aisle. A conservative commentator on Fox News, Charles Krauthammer, was really hitting me hard last spring. He couldn't believe I was #1 in the polls and kept knocking me. Now, you have to understand, he didn't know me, he never met me. But one day on Bill O'Reilly's show, Krauthammer hit me so hard it was ridiculous. He said mine was a joke candidacy or something to that effect. So O'Reilly sent Jesse Watters to New Hampshire to get my response. I let Krauthammer have it. I was very tough, some would say vicious, but I was tough because Krauthammer had been tough to me.

The next day I turned on the show and they didn't air my response. I called O'Reilly and said, "Bill, what happened? Krauthammer can talk about me but I can't talk about him?" Bill gave me what I considered a weak reason as to why he wouldn't play my response and I left it at that. I think Bill O'Reilly is terrific, and I think Greta Van Susteren, Sean Hannity, and Neil Cavuto are as well. These are outstanding people who get big ratings and do a fantastic job. But in this case I thought Bill was wrong. I should have been allowed to rebut Krauthammer as a matter of fairness.

In any case, there's a reason Fox News has such high quality programs and phenomenal ratings. His name is Roger Ailes. Whether some people like it or not, Roger Ailes, the creator of Fox News, working together with Rupert Murdoch, is one of the great geniuses in television history. Roger can look at a person and instantly tell whether that individual will grab ratings. In addition to O'Reilly, Van Susteren, Hannity, and Cavuto, Roger has numerous others who do amazing work. People like Bret Baier. I also love the team on *Fox and Friends* with Gretchen Carlson, Steve Doocy, and Brian Kilmeade. They're smart, quick, funny, and really know what's going on. The Fox morning show is a tremendous success due to its three talented hosts and the wonderful Roger Ailes. I really enjoy being on it.

Guys like Ailes understand that ratings rule. When I have friends with television shows that aren't doing well, they just can't understand why they're being canceled. I tell them this: I have learned that entertainment is a very simple business. You can be a horrible human being, you can be a truly terrible person, but if you get ratings, you are a king. If you don't get ratings, you are immediately canceled and nothing else will matter.

I happen to get ratings, and always have. Larry King used to tell me, "You get the highest ratings." Everybody wants me to be on their show, not because they like me, not because I'm handsome and have great hair, but because I get ratings. To tell you the truth, I'm not exactly sure why. I don't want to be provocative, and in many cases I try not to be provocative. But I think the reason millions of people follow my views on world events is because they know I understand that our country is being ripped off by OPEC, China, and other countries. They know America is in big trouble if we don't get back on the right track. And they know I'm not afraid to tell it like it is. It's not that they like or love me—it's that they respect what I have to say, believe the same thing themselves, and know that I'm right.

I'm also told that many people have a general interest in the details of my life and the people I work with in show business, particularly since they've seen all the amazing talent I've had on *Celebrity Apprentice*. It's always fun to see the kinds of questions people ask in the letters and emails my office receives. I enjoy working with stars and seeing their careers grow.

One of the most interesting and special people I've gotten to know is Lady Gaga. About five years ago, when she was a total unknown, Lady Gaga was the entertainment for the Miss Universe Pageant, which was held that year in Vietnam. I own the Miss Universe Pageant and have made it very, very successful. One day my people came to me and told me about a young woman they called Lady Gaga who nobody had ever heard of. We put her on as the entertainer in the middle of the pageant, which is broadcast internationally. I thought, "Wow, she is really, really good." The next day, it was crazy. Everybody was talking about how good Lady Gaga was— "Who is she, where is she? She's going to be someone big, she's amazing!" Well, she became a big star and maybe she became a star because I put her on the Miss Universe Pageant. It's very possible, who knows what would have happened without it, because she caused a sensation.

A couple years later, she opened in New York and was hotter than ever at Radio City Music Hall. I was there and happened to be sitting with a large group of very major celebrities. I won't mention their names because I'm not looking to embarrass anybody. Gaga gave a fantastic performance and, after she was finished, her manager came and shouted, "Mr. Trump, Gaga wants to see you, but only you, nobody else can come." Now, here you have major singers, musicians, and television personalities and the manager is shouting to me, "Mr. Trump, only you and nobody else." I went back with my wife, Melania, and talked to Lady Gaga for about forty-five minutes. She's a fantastic person, solid as a rock, and I'm very proud of her success because I really believe I had at least something to do with it.

No matter if you're talking about media from the entertainment world or news shows, the media bookers all try to get me on their programs to help boost their ratings. Because I operate in both entertainment TV and current events shows, I have a keen understanding of how various moves affect ratings. For instance, I told Jeff Zucker, who previously ran NBC, "Jeff, don't move Jay Leno. He's #1 in the evening and when you are #1, you don't move. In fact, not only is he #1, he is a strong #1. Don't move Jay Leno—it is a terrible mistake."

I warned them that it would be the first time in history somebody's going to be taken out of the #1 position and moved and told them it would turn Leno into the equivalent of a lame duck president. In any event, they did it and Conan went on. To put it mildly, it didn't work. Jay went back to his original time and has never been the same again. His show's ratings are way down from what they were—he has never fully recovered.

I was actually doing the *Jay Leno Show* the night he was told that this move was going to be made and, even though it wasn't going to take place for five years, I could see that he was devastated, confused, and didn't know why they were doing it. I didn't either. It turned out to be possibly the greatest mistake in broadcast history.

Politics and television are nasty businesses. When the two collide, things get even nastier. As an example, Jay Leno—he knocks the hell out of me on the show but always wants me to be on. The interesting thing is, even the ones that really go after me want me on the show for one reason and one reason only: I am a ratings machine.

Still, no matter how good your ratings are, sometimes you can't stop the press from running stories that are totally false but that they know will grab viewers or readers. To show you how dishonest the press is, I recently sold a house for $7.15 million. It was a house I had built at my great Trump National Golf Club in Los Angeles. The home is in a beautiful location fronting the Pacific Ocean with views of the course. This house was originally built for someone else who was unable to get financing from our country's wonderful banks and defaulted on $1.5 million. The house, which is one of seventy-five lots I own facing the ocean, cost me very little above that amount, so I had the house for almost nothing.

I listed the house for $12 million knowing I couldn't get anywhere near that but figuring it's a great way to negotiate. The buyer paid me $7.15 million, which was a substantial profit on that individual parcel.

The dishonest press smelled blood. Headlines raged that I had taken a major haircut on my home, as if I were selling my own *personal* house, not one of many in the development. In actuality, I had only been inside the house one time for five minutes to check it out. But it didn't matter. We tried to correct the newspapers, but the *Los Angeles Times* and others got the story totally wrong. In fact, one reporter told one of my lawyers that he knew we were right, that it wasn't my personal house, and that he knew the sale was almost all profit.

"So why did you write it that way?" my lawyer asked. "Because it doesn't make for a good story," the reporter told him. That's how dishonest the press can be.

The Presidency

In all my years in business and participating in politics I've never seen the country as divided as it is right now—and I've seen bad times. Voters' hatred of both Democrats and Republicans is beyond anything I have ever witnessed. A great leader can bring America together. But unfortunately for us, Barack Obama is not a leader. So who can the country turn to?

I have been saying for a long time that it is very hard for a truly successful person to run for political office. Your rivals and the press will take every deal you've ever made, even the best of them, and make them look bad. You could have built a $7 billion+ net worth, but it doesn't make any difference, because they will make you look as foolish as possible. A guy like Obama has it much easier. He had never done a deal before except for the purchase of his house which, in my opinion, was not an honest transaction. A smart investigative reporter should definitely look into that because any objective examination of the facts reveals there was definitely something fishy going on. But that was the only deal Obama ever did. He hasn't done hundreds of deals like very successful people do, where we employ thousands of people and have to manage numerous complex enterprises. So he had an easier go of it.

Mark Burnett, my good friend, partner, and the best producer in television, really wanted me to continue with *The Apprentice* and not run for president. Mark's big shows are *The Apprentice*, *Survivor*, and now the hit show *The Voice*. He said, "Donald, I think you would be an incredible

president, but you are far too successful to run. You've done too many deals
and too many things. They'll go after every single deal you've ever done
and, even on the best of them, will try to make you look bad."

So essentially, Mark was voicing what I had been saying for the last two
years—that a very successful person cannot run for political office (especially the presidency) and isn't that sad, because that's the kind of person
and thinking we need to bring the country back.

Either way, when I was leading in the polls, I committed an unforced error.
I was asked by a friend to make a speech in Las Vegas in front of a small group.
I agreed. A couple hundred people were expected, mostly Republican women,
and it was no big deal. Or so I thought. But when they announced that I was
going to speak, thousands of people showed up. The owner of the hotel, a great
man named Phil Ruffin, one of the smartest investors around, told me it was
the most people they had ever packed into the ballroom at the hotel. The place
was mobbed. Everybody was happy. They were thrilled, and in the room you
had lots of good, tough Las Vegas people who I can't believe will ever vote for
Obama, especially after he told people not to go to Las Vegas.

We had thousands of people there, it turned out to be wild, and I made
a mistake. I catered to that crowd. They absolutely loved the speech and I
used some foul language which, with that crowd, went over phenomenally
well. But unfortunately they had cameras in the room, which I didn't see,
and only those parts of the speech where I used strong language ended up
being shown through our nation.

I wish I hadn't done it. It got a lot of press but some people were turned
off by it. I'm not a big curser but it did take place, and I will say the people
in the room loved that speech, because we're not living in a baby world.

It's a rough, mean world where everybody's out to get everybody else and where other countries are out to get the United States, and they are doing a pretty good job of it. So I got fired up and the crowd did too.

Of course, Joe Biden dropped the f-word in front of the entire media on a stage with the president. But Biden gets a pass because he's with Obama, and as we all know, Obama can do no wrong in the media's eyes.

In my opinion, our president is totally overrated both as a person and as a campaigner. The press has given a false impression of him as a brilliant student (which he was not), a brilliant leader (which he is not), and a campaigner the likes of which we have not seen in many years. Yet now many Democrats are suffering buyer's remorse and wish they had elected Hillary Clinton instead.

Regardless, the Republicans are going to have a very tough race. Obama is harnessing all of the negativity he created and flipping it back on the people—a very smart, if cynical, strategy. I've never seen anything like it. The guy is willing to rip the country in half to win. Sadly, it may prove to be a winning strategy. If I were doing as badly as he is, I would realize it is my only road to victory.

I love my life and businesses, so I would rather not run for president. When people say I should run as an Independent, I remind them that it's very hard for an Independent to win, though perhaps easier than ever before. Still, if the economy continues to be bad (which I think it will, due to incompetent leadership) and Republicans pick the wrong candidate (which I hope they won't), I can't completely rule out a run. Most people have never heard of a very stupid law—called equal time—that prevents someone with a major television show from running for political office. So Obama is allowed to go on television every day and can fly around the country any time he wants at taxpayer expense, but I'm not allowed to do *The Apprentice* and run for office at the same time. You tell me, is that right? Were it not for that ridiculous law I would probably be running for president right now and having a good time doing it—because America has tremendous potential, unbelievable potential, and it is being wasted.

I distinctly remember when I made my decision to sign for another season of *The Apprentice*, which put my run for the presidency on hold. It was a Friday about 7:00 p.m., and Melania was watching *Entertainment Tonight*, *Access Hollywood*, *Extra*, or one of the various entertainment shows she enjoys and frankly so do I. I sat down at the dinner table with the television blaring and watched as some of the biggest actors and actresses in Hollywood were hoping that their networks would pick up their show for another season. You see, the following Monday, NBC was having its big "Upfront" where they and the other networks announce their schedules for the year. So this was a tough time for actors because they wanted to know if their shows were going to be renewed.

As Melania and I were watching, I'm seeing these big stars saying, "I hope they renew our show, our show is so great, our cast is so amazing, the ratings are okay." Everything was, "I hope, I hope, I hope," and I'm watching these major actors almost begging. That's when I said to my wife, "You know, baby, it's amazing. I have a show that is a big success and I have the president of the network calling me all day long saying, 'Donald, Donald, we want you, we love you.'" In addition to that, I had a great guy named

Steve Burke at Comcast saying to me something like, "Donald, we'd like you to renew, we'd like you to go for another season or whatever you want, please renew." So I am saying to myself, here these network executives are calling me on an hourly basis wanting me to renew my contract for another season of a two-hour hit show on primetime Sunday, and I am telling them no and yet I come home and I watch the entertainment shows and all of these big name actors and actresses are hoping beyond hope that they are going to be renewed. At that precise moment I got a call from Steve Burke reiterating the fact that they would love to have me sign the contract. Right then and there I said to my wife, "Baby, you know what? This is ridiculous. I'm going to sign the contract with NBC."

My wife, Melania, who is considered by many, including me, to be one of the most beautiful women in the world, has amazing instincts. For years I would ask her whether or not I could run and win. And she would say, "Donald, people love you, but they wouldn't vote for you for president." When I asked her why, she said, "You're a little wild and a little too con-troversial. They respect you, they think you're really smart—the smartest of all—but enough people just wouldn't vote for you."

So she told me this for a long period of time and then recently, as she's watching political news on television and seeing all the things that are wrong with our country, she looks at me and says, "Darling, you know you'd win if you ran, don't you?" I said, "What do you mean? You always told me I couldn't win." She said, "But now you could win, and maybe even easily. People really want you. I see it on the streets. People want you and they really need you."

This was a great compliment coming from a very smart woman.

Some people have yet to realize how serious I was and am about running for the White House. In fact I was so close that I had already prepared the Public Financial Disclosure Report required of a presidential candidate. That's a big deal because the Trump Organization is a private company, and people don't know what I'm really worth. So I had the independent firm Predictive, which is used by government agencies and top companies like GM, Visa, Pfizer, and others, prepare valuations on branding, and we filled out the other areas of the long and complex presidential Public Financial Disclosure Report. So my forms were already completed when I told NBC I'd renew. I was ready to sign and submit the papers, which were completed in strict compliance with the instructions. Rather than waste the forms (and who knows, I may be filing them sometime later), I thought I would share the most important three pages with you in this book. These are three of the many pages of the completed submittal. The third summary page is probably the most important.

My primary reason for running for the presidency would be to straighten out the mess Obama has made of our country. I have built a truly great company, one with unbelievable assets and locations that I believe are about as good as it gets. We have great asset value, cash flow, and very little debt. I want the American people to see this, because ultimately our country is, in a certain way, the exact *opposite* of my company. And whether it's me or someone else, we need the kind of thinking that can produce this kind of success. For the sophisticated financial people who already know me, these numbers come as no surprise. For the miserable, petty, jealous wannabes who knowingly fabricate stories about me, maybe this will shut them up.

SF 278 (Rev. 03/2000)
5 CFR Part 2634
U.S. Office of Government Ethics

Executive Branch Personnel PUBLIC FINANCIAL DISCLOSURE REPORT

Form Approved:
OMB No. 3209 - 0001

	Reporting Status (Check Appropriate Boxes)	Incumbent	Calendar Year Covered by Report	New Entrant, Nominee, or Candidate	Termination Filer	Termination Date (If Applicable) (Month, Day, Year)
Dated of Appointment, Candidacy, Election, or Nomination (Month, Day, Year)		☐		☒	☐	

Reporting Individual's Name

Last Name	First Name and Middle Initial
Trump	Donald J

Position for Which Filing

Title of Position	Department or Agency (If Applicable)
President of the United States	

Location of Present Office (or forwarding address)

Address (Number, Street, City, State , and ZIP Code)	Telephone No. (Include Area Code)
725 Fifth Avenue, New York, NY 10022	212-832-2000

Position(s) Held with the Federal Government During the Preceding 12 Months (If Not Same as Above)

N/A

Title of Position(s) and Date(s) Held

Presidential Nominees Subject to Senate Confirmation

Not Applicable

Name of Congressional Committee Considering Nomination	Do You Intend to Create a Qualified Diversified Trust
	☐ Yes ☐ No

Certification

I CERTIFY that the statements I have made on this form and all attached schedules are true, complete and correct to the best of my knowledge.

Signature of Reporting Individual	Date (Month, Day, Year)

Other Review (If desired by agency)

Signature of Other Reviewer	Date (Month, Day, Year)

Agency/Ethics Official's Opinion

On the basis of information contained in this report, I conclude that the filer is in compliance with applicable laws and regulations (subject to any comment in the box below).

Signature of Designated Agency Ethics Official/Reviewing Official	Date (Month, Day, Year)

Office of Government Ethics Use Only

Signature	Date (Month, Day, Year)

Comments of Reviewing Officials (If additional space is required, use the reverse side of this sheet)

☐ (Check box if filing extension granted & indicate number of days ———)

☐ (Check box if comments are continued on the reverse side)

Fee for Late Filing

Any individual who is required to file this report and does so more than 30 days after the date the report is required to be filed, or, if an extension is granted, more than 30 days after the last day of the filing extension period, shall be subject to a $200 fee.

Reporting Periods

Incumbents: The reporting period is the preceding calendar year except Part II of Schedule C and Part I of Schedule D where you must also include the filing year up to the date you file. Part II of Schedule D is not applicable.

Termination Filers: The reporting period is the preceding calendar year and the current calendar year up to the date covered by your previous filing and ends at the date of termination. Part II of Schedule D is not applicable.

Nominees, New Entrants and Candidates for President and Vice President:

Schedule A–The reporting period for income (BLOCK C) is the preceding calendar year and the current calendar year up to the date of filing. Value assets as of any date you choose that is within 31 days of the date of filing.

Schedule B–Not applicable.

Schedule C, Part I (Liabilities)–The reporting period is the preceding calendar year and the current calendar year up to any date you choose that is within 31 days of the date of filing.

Schedule C, Part II (Agreements or Arrangements)–Show any agreements or arrangements as of the date of filing.

Schedule D–The reporting period is the preceding two calendar years and the current calendar year up to the date of filing.

Agency Use Only	OGE Use Only

SF 278 (Rev. 03/2000)
5 C.F.R. Part 2634
U.S. Office of Government Ethics

Reporting Individual's Name		Page Number
Trump, Donald J	SCHEDULE A	2 of

Assets and Income

BLOCK A	Valuation of Assets at close of reporting period — BLOCK B	Income: type and amount. If "None (or less than $201)" is checked, no other entry is needed in Block C for that item. — BLOCK C

For you, your spouse, and dependent children, report each asset held for investment or the production of income which had a fair market value exceeding $1,000 at the close of the reporting period, or which generated more than $200 in income during the reporting period, together with such income.

For yourself, also report the source and actual amount of earned income exceeding $200 (other than from the U.S. Government). For your spouse, report the source but not the amount of earned income of more than $1,000 (except report the actual amount of any honoraria over $200 of your spouse).

None ☐

BLOCK B — Valuation of Assets at close of reporting period (columns):
None (or less than $1,001) / $1,001 - $15,000 / $15,001 - $50,000 / $50,001 - $100,000 / $100,001 - $250,000 / $250,001 - $500,000 / $500,001 - $1,000,000 / Over $1,000,000* / $1,000,001 - $5,000,000 / $5,000,001 - $25,000,000 / $25,000,001 - $50,000,000 / Over $50,000,000 / Excepted Investment Fund / Excepted Trust / Qualified Trust

BLOCK C — Income Type: Dividends / Rent and Royalties / Interest / Capital Gains
Income Amount: None (or less than $201) / $201 - $1,000 / $1,001 - $2,500 / $2,501 - $5,000 / $5,001 - $15,000 / $15,001 - $50,000 / $50,001 - $100,000 / $100,001 - $1,000,000 / Over $1,000,000* / $1,000,001 - $5,000,000 / Over $5,000,000 / Other Income (Specify Type & Actual Amount) / Date (Mo., Day, Yr.) Only if Honoraria

Examples:

	Valuation (Block B)	Income Type	Income Amount
General Atlantic Common	$15,001 - $50,000	Dividends	$1,001 - $2,500
Doe/Jones & Smith, Hometown, State	$100,001 - $250,000; Excepted Investment Fund	—	$2,501 - $5,000
Xampptous Equity Fund	$500,001 - $1,000,000; Excepted Investment Fund	—	$5,001 - $15,000
RE: Heartland 500 Index Fund	$100,001 - $250,000	—	Other Income: Law Partnership Income $130,000

Assets:

#	Asset / Income	Valuation (Block B)	Income (Block C)
1	Capital One Bank New York, NY; Checking Account (See attached)	$5,000,001 - $25,000,000	None (or less than $201)
2	Capital One Bank New York, NY; Money Market Account (See attached)	$5,000,001 - $25,000,000	None (or less than $201)
3	JPMorgan Chase Bank New York, NY Checking Account (See attached)	$5,000,001 - $25,000,000	None (or less than $201)
4	JP Morgan Bank New York, NY; Checking Account (See attached)	$5,000,001 - $25,000,000	$1,001 - $2,500
5	Bank of America, New York, NY; Savings Account (See attached)	$25,000,001 - $50,000,000	$5,001 - $15,000
6	Citibank, New York, NY; Money Market Account (See attached)	$5,000,001 - $25,000,000	$201 - $1,000

* This category applies only if the asset/income is solely that of the filer's spouse or dependent children. If the asset/income is either that of the filer or jointly held by the filer with the spouse or dependent children, mark the other higher categories of value, as appropriate

Prior Editions Cannot Be Used.

Donald J. Trump
Summary of Net Worth
As of June 30, 2010

ASSETS

Cash & Marketable Securities - as reflected herein is after
the acquisition of numerous assets (i.e. multiple aircraft,
golf courses, etc), the paying off of significant
mortgages for cash and before the collection of
significant receivables (see schedule attached)   270,300,000

Real & Operating Properties owned 100% by Donald J. Trump
through various entities controlled by him:
Commercial Properties (New York City)   1,370,650,000

Residential Properties (New York City)   348,450,000

Club facilities & related real estate   1,220,000,000

Properties under development   261,000,000

Real Properties owned less than 100% by Donald J. Trump
1290 Avenue of the Americas - New York City
Bank of America Building - San Francisco, California
and others
Total Value Net of Debt   652,200,000

Real Estate Licensing Deals   107,800,000

Miss Universe, Miss USA and Miss Teen USA Pageants   20,000,000

Other Assets (net of debt)   133,160,000

Brand Value (See Note below)   3,000,000,000
Total Assets   7,383,560,000

LIABILITIES

Accounts payable   4,900,000

Loans and mortgages payable on Real and Operating
Properties as reflected above   373,760,000
Total Liabilities   378,660,000

NET WORTH   7,004,900,000

Note

Mr. Trump's Brand Value has been estimated at $3Billion and is reflected herein. The Brand Value has
been established by Predictiv, the highly respected brand valuation company. Predictiv assists Global
500 corporations and government agencies to improve management performance, marketing and
strategy. Predictiv measures the financial impact of intangibles such as brand, strategy execution,
innovation and post-merger integration. Clients have included Southwest Air, Pfizer, Petrobras,
General Motors, UPS, United Technologies, BASF, Visa and Major League Baseball.

By the way, in the spirit of transparency, these forms were completed *before* the very public purchase of the late billionaire John Kluge's winery, which became embroiled in controversy and tens of millions of dollars of debt after his divorce. Now called the Trump Vineyard Estates, the winery is located in one of the best areas in the United States, Charlottesville, Virginia. Trump Vineyard Estates is more than 1,000 acres and has already received a great amount of publicity in the Washington and Virginia press and was featured on the cover of *Town & Country* magazine. Originally, it cost around $150 million to build and assemble. I bought it at auction for $6.2 million in cash. I pride myself on being liquid when few others are. That's one of the reasons I was able to buy the Kluge estate for such a terrific price—cash. There were many people at the foreclosure auction who knew what an amazing asset it was, but they didn't have the cash or would need bank financing at a much higher amount to close the deal. By the way, the reason I have so much cash is that, among other things, I've made some of the best branding deals around, especially recently. If our government were as wise with our nation's cash, we wouldn't be in the big mess we are in today.

Some people think the presidency no longer matters, that the United States is finished. But let me tell you, the president makes all the difference in the world. If we get the right president, our country can become stronger and better and more successful than ever before.

The Republican field has several good candidates in the race—most of whom have come to see me at my office in Trump Tower. The reason they come to see me isn't just because I am a nice person but because millions of people listen to what I say and know I "get it." Some magazines have said I am the single most important endorsement a presidential candidate can have. I don't know if that's true but it wouldn't surprise me. I don't say that to brag, I just tell it like it is.

It started when Sarah Palin came to Trump Tower. She is a terrific woman and gets an unfair shake from the media. We had a great conversation. She said, "Hey, let's go out for pizza." We did and it was bedlam, with tons of people swarming us. I got criticized because I ate my pizza with a fork. (The truth is, I know how to eat pizza but I was trying to eat as little as possible because I hate gaining weight!) But I really enjoyed my time with Sarah and her family. We caused quite a stir on the streets of New York and especially in front of that pizza parlor. It was wild!

Michele Bachmann came up to my office more than once. She is a real worker bee. She started low, shot to the top of the polls, and then dropped down again, probably because Rick Perry came in and stole a lot of her thunder. But Michele is a wonderful person and no matter what happens with her run for the White House she's got a great political future ahead of her. She's passionate about America and a strong protector of traditional values.

When Rick Perry came to see me at Trump Tower we had a great discussion, and then went to Jean Georges Restaurant, probably the best restaurant in New York, which is located on the street level of Trump International Hotel and Tower at One Central Park West. We had an incredible conversation and I found him to be a good and personable guy, much different from what you see in the debates. Since then, I have spoken to him on numerous occasions, and every time I speak to him he is so forceful and strong that I have actually said to him: "Rick, why can't you act this way during the debates?" He said, "Donald, the debates are just not my thing." So I said, "Why don't you pretend you are someplace else?

You gotta act different. You are getting killed in the debates." But he repeated, "Donald, they are just not for me." Fair enough. But Rick was severely hurt by what took place in the debates. It was sad to see. The debates are turning out to be much more important in this presidential cycle than in past primaries, and if you don't do well in the debates, it's a long climb back to the top. But again, Rick is a terrific guy with some solid ideas. It will be interesting to see if he can regain his footing.

Mitt Romney came up to Trump Tower. I had never met Mitt before and, not having met him, maybe I was inclined not to be in his corner. The fact is, when you meet him in person, he is a much different guy than he is in public. He is warm and engaging. The public has to get to know him better. He gets criticized for changing his opinions, or "flip flopping," but over a lifetime I've seen many people who don't change and they always get left behind. Smart people learn things, so they change their minds. Only stupid people never change their minds.

In the debates, Mitt has been spectacular. He's sharp, highly educated, and looks like a president. The amazing thing is, no matter how well he does, no matter who endorses him, he seems to stay at about the same numbers in the polls. *So far*, although he remains at the top or close to the top in the polls, he seems frozen at around 25 percent of primary voters. As other candidates drop out of the race, those numbers may break in his favor. Only time will tell.

Herman Cain is a real piece of work. He came up to my office and immediately I liked him and I believe he liked me. He's a terrific guy with a magnetic personality (he also happens to be a great singer). When Herman left Trump Tower, the press swarmed over him and I was told he said something like, "Look, I don't know if I am going to get Donald's support or endorsement but I wanted to get to know him and I wanted him to like me because he's got the most vicious mouth for anybody he doesn't like and I didn't want him badmouthing me." I thought it was extremely cute and honest and I do indeed like Herman Cain. He's run an amazing campaign with very little staff. That has some advantages. There are plenty of political bloodsuckers who leech on to candidates and get millions of dollars and do nothing but give the candidates bad ideas and bad advice.

One thing I told Herman is that no matter what happens, he has elevated his stock. If he doesn't win, which is a very distinct possibility, he can run for another office and walk in. Whether it's the Senate or a governorship or even running a company, Herman has built a great resume and done it for peanuts. He didn't waste money—and I really admire that.

As this book goes to press, there are some vicious rumors swirling around Herman. These kinds of charges are to be expected in any political race, but we will see if he can weather them.

One mistake I made was with Jon Huntsman who really seems like a nice guy. He called me a number of times and I was unbelievably busy doing a deal and I didn't get back to him. Then, the time got long enough that I decided maybe I shouldn't bother him.

Jon Huntsman and his family have done an amazing job for the Wharton School of Finance, which is the best business school in the world. We both went there and I respect him and the job his family has done. Nevertheless, when all the candidates were saying they were coming up to see me, he said just the opposite. He said, "I don't have to see Donald

Trump. I don't need Donald Trump. I don't want to see Donald Trump."
What he didn't say was that he called me to have a meeting. While I like
Jon Huntsman, he should not have said he didn't call me when he did. In
fact, he left me his number and the person's name to call to set up a meeting. If you want, I can give you both. I know he won't lie if directly asked
about this. I should have called him back—it wasn't polite and to him I
apologize. If he ever calls again I promise to take his call and I would look
forward to meeting him. With that said, for many more reasons which are
fairly obvious, he can't and won't win the presidency in 2012.

One group that has already won is the Tea Party. The Tea Party has
done a great service to the United States. They have made all politicians
look seriously at what's wrong with our country, including America's
$15 trillion of debt.

The media continuously bash the Tea Party. Nothing could be more
unfair. In fact, when the Tea Party held a rally recently in Richmond, Virginia, they were forced to put up $10,000 to take care of insurance and
barricades—and they gladly did it. When Occupy Wall Street marched,
their gathering caused much more disturbance and disruption and they
weren't asked to put up any money. The press constantly maligns, ridicules,
and mocks the Tea Party folks. The fact is the Tea Party is made up of great
citizens of this country. And in the end, I think the Tea Party patriots will
get the last laugh because they will go down as having done more to change
the country than any other group. They are terrific people, great Americans, and I am proud to have such a good relationship with them.

As for the Occupy Wall Street protesters, I am certainly not opposed
to them or their concerns, some of which are legitimate. They are angry at

the banks and they should be. They are angry at the government and they have every right to be. But, as I tell them all the time when they call my office, they need to move their protest over to the White House and get the community organizer out of his 747 and into the Oval Office so he can get to work making good deals with other countries and stopping other nations from ripping us off. If we could take back our jobs and money from China, OPEC, and all of the other places that are ripping us off, we wouldn't have to decimate our safety net and leave those who really need help stranded. That's a cause worth fighting for.

Of course, while there are some Occupy protesters who are serious and sincere people, there are a lot of them who are just there to meet people and have a party. And there are still others who are bad people who are involved for bad reasons. What started as a protest is becoming dangerous to the protesters. How long it will last is anyone's guess.

One thing the Tea Party folks and the Occupy Wall Street people can and should agree on is tackling the rampant problem in the Obama administration of *crony capitalism*. We've already seen with Solyndra and Fisker how the president's pals and big time campaign donors all got sweetheart loans and deals and stuck taxpayers with the bill. I predict we haven't heard the last of it and that the Obama administration engaged in many more cases of funneling money to companies connected to the president and his donors. Mark my word.

I love capitalism enough to protect it. There has to be a level playing field where everyone can compete fairly. The guy swinging a hammer all day shouldn't have the government reaching in his pocket and handing his taxes to Obama's big shot donors. It's wrong and unfair. Teachers, nurses, police officers, and firefighters have no business bailing out Wall Street bankers and billion-dollar companies.

Likewise, I think the Occupy people and the Tea Party can agree to get rid of the corporate welfare that gives tax subsidies to oil companies. How does that make any sense? Oil companies make billions. Why should the taxpayers have money taken out of their hard-earned paycheck to hand over to the oil companies, many of whom are in cahoots with OPEC? That's stupid and unfair as anyone can clearly see.

I believe America can restore herself to greatness. But we need the right kind of change to tap the massive potential locked inside our great country. The so-called "ruling class" in Washington needs to be replaced with people committed to the Constitution and the values of fair play, hard work, and sparking the innovation and entrepreneurship that has made America great.

We just lost a great innovator and American entrepreneur in Steve Jobs. Like his politics or not, Jobs changed the world with his technological innovations. Interestingly, Jobs kept Washington money largely out of Apple—he wanted his company to stand and fight on its own two feet. Jobs, who was an Obama supporter, had a great idea that he offered to the president. "Put together a group of six or seven CEOs who could really explain the innovation challenges in America." But according to Walter Isaacson's biography of Jobs, once the White House officials got involved they messed it up, trying to micromanage things and turning it into a much larger event, and Steve Jobs pulled out.[1]

We need more innovators, dreamers, and entrepreneurs. America used to be #1 in producing all three. We can restore America and unleash the incredible potential of our great land and people. All it takes is the wisdom to return to our core principles, the resolve to keep the faith, and the willingness to get tough and innovate.

Take, for example, the X-PRIZE Foundation. This entrepreneurial group hosts competitions with cash prizes for the most innovative idea in Education, Exploration, Energy, and Life Sciences. The first $10 million reward was given in 2004 to whatever team could launch a manned spacecraft twice in two weeks. The X-PRIZE motto is totally American: "Revolution Through Competition."[2] That's the way Americans like to think. That's the American Dream in motion. We're going to have to invent our way out of the mess our country is in. It starts with doing something I've always done, which is to think big.

Americans dream big and do hard things. It's who we are. It's what we do. When our country is unchained, we're unstoppable. But we need smart leaders, people who understand how the world works and have the guts to get tough. With proper leadership, we can rebuild the shining city on a hill we once were. When we do, we should boldly and proudly celebrate America's power and dominance in the world. The way I see it, greatness need not apologize for itself. Ever.

If we do that, we can, together, make America #1 again.

ACKNOWLEDGMENTS

The team at Regnery Publishing has been terrific to work with in every way, and I'd like to thank Wynton Hall, Peter Schweizer, Marji Ross, Jeff Carneal, and Harry Crocker for doing such a great job. They've been a pleasure to work with and their professionalism was apparent from the start. At the Trump Organization I would like to thank Rhona Graff, Meredith McIver, Michael Cohen, Kacey Kennedy, and Thuy Colayco for their enthusiasm and careful work. Thanks to all for a job well done.

NOTES

Chapter One

1. Sara Murray, "About 1 in 7 in U.S. Receive Food Stamps," *Wall Street Journal*, Real Time Economics, May 3, 2011.
2. "Wholesale Prices Spike on Steep Rise in Food, Oil," Associated Press, March 16, 2011, http://abcnews.go.com/Business/wireStory?id =13146470.
3. Tom Shanker and David E. Sanger, "U.S. to Aid South Korea With Naval Defense Plan," *New York Times*, May 30, 2010, http://www.nytimes.com/2010/05/31/world/asia/31koreanavy.html?page wanted=2.

Chapter Two

1. F. Michael Maloof, "Guess which country kicked out U.S. congressional delegation," *WorldNetDaily*, June 18, 2011, http://www.wnd.com/?pageId=312317.
2. GAO Report No. GAO-10-304, "Iraqi-U.S. Cost-Sharing: Iraq Has a Cumulative Budget Surplus, Offering the Potential for Further Cost-Sharing," Government Accountability Office, September 13, 2010; accessible text file available at: http://www.gao.gov/htext/d10304.html.

3.   Jim Geraghty, "Obama: On gas prices, 'I would have preferred a gradual adjust-ment,'" National Review Online *The Campaign Spot*, June 11, 2008, http://www.nationalreview.com/campaign-spot/9477/obama-gas-prices-i-would-have-preferred-gradual-adjustment.

4.   Neil King Jr. and Stephen Power, "Times Tough for Energy Overhaul," *Wall Street Journal*, December 12, 2008, http://online.wsj.com/article/SB122904040307499791.html.

5.   Posted by Ed Morrissey, "Obama: I'll make energy prices 'skyrocket,'" HotAir.com, November 2, 2008 http://hotair.com/archives/2008/11/02/obama-ill-make-energy-prices-skyrocket/.

6.   Jeff Cox, "Gas Prices May Be Falling, But Food Keeps Going Up," CNBC.com, June 23, 2011, http://www.cnbc.com/id/43498072.

7.   Lucia Graves, "Obama Says He Has No Regrets About Solyndra Loan," *Huffington Post*, October 3, 2011, http://www.huffingtonpost.com/2011/10/03/obama-solyndra-loan_n_993085.html.

8.   Brad Plumer, "Five myths about the Solyndra collapse," *Washington Post*, Septem-ber 14, 2011, http://www.washingtonpost.com/blogs/ezra -klein/post/five-myths-about-the-solyndra-collapse/2011/09/14/gIQA fkyvRK_blog.html.

9.   Lucia Graves, "Obama Says He Has No Regrets About Solyndra Loan," *Huffington Post*, October 3, 2011, http://www.huffingtonpost.com/2011/10/03/obama-solyndra-loan_n_993085.html

10. Brad Plumer, "Five myths about the Solyndra collapse," *Washington Post*, Septem-ber 14, 2011, http://www.washingtonpost.com/blogs/ezra -klein/post/five-myths-about-the-solyndra-collapse/2011/09/14/gIQA fkyvRK_blog.html.

11. "Hugo Chavez Mouthpiece Says U.S. Hit Haiti With 'Earthquake Weapon,'" FOXNews.com, January 21, 2010, http://www.foxnews.com/world/2010/01/21/hugo-chavez-mouthpiece-says-hit-haiti-earthquake-weapon/.

12. Rob Hastings, "Saudi Arabia is 'biggest funder of terrorists,'" *The Independent*, December 6, 2010, http://www.independent.co.uk/news/world/middle-east/saudi-arabia-is-biggest-funder-of-terrorists-2152327.html.

13. Thomas W. Evans, "Sue OPEC," New York Times, June 19, 2008, http://www.nytimes.com/2008/06/19/opinion/19evans.html.

14. Robert Zubrin, "Obama Covers for OPEC," op. cit.

15. Thomas W. Evans, "Sue OPEC," op. cit.

16. Ibid.

17. Khawaja Mohammad Hasan, Abu Dhabi, "Cheap, clean & green transport initia-tive," Khaleej Times Online, January 30, 2011, http://www.khaleejtimes.com/DisplayArticle08.asp?xfile=/data/openspace/2011/January/openspace_January29.xml&section=openspace.

18. Rob Lever, "Amid US gas boom, split over 'fracking,'" AFP, June 26, 2011, http://www.google.com/hostednews/afp/article/ALeqM5j_sM -PZ5NWAybKbWdOM poXvh67ng?docId=CNG.bb9547c e35c8697828233d280f68bf54.291.

19. David Ropeik, "How Risky Is It, Really?" *Psychology Today*, May 31, 2010, http://www.psychologytoday.com/blog/how-risky-is-it-really/201005/it-s-not-just-about-oil-in-the-ocean-it-s-how-it-got-there.

20. "Natural sources of marine oil pollution," GPA, http://oils.gpa.unep.org/facts/natural-sources.htm.

21. "Top 10 Proofs Obama Wants High Energy Prices," *Human Events*, June 20, 2011, p. 19.

Chapter Three

1. Transcript, "The Democrats' First 2008 Presidential Debate," *New York Times*, April 27, 2007, http://www.nytimes.com/2007/04/27/us/politics/27debate_transcript.html?pagewanted=print.

2. Kathy Chu, "Most Americans think China is No. 1 economy; it isn't," *USA Today*, February 15, 2011, http://www.usatoday.com/money/economy/2011-02-14-chinapoll14_ST_N.htm.

3. "The China Job Drain," Alliance for American Manufacturing, http://www.americanmanufacturing.org/china-job-loss.

4. Gideon Rachman, "Think Again: American Decline," *Foreign Policy*, January/February 2011, http://www.foreignpolicy.com/articles/ 2011/01/02/think_again_american_decline.

5. Ibid., and Graeme Wearden, "US-China trade deficit grows to record $27obn," *The Guardian*, February 11, 2011, http://www.guardian.co.uk/business/2011/feb/11/us-chinese-trade-gap-grows.

6. Peter Navarro, "How China unfairly bests the U.S.," *Los Angeles Times*, June 21, 2011, http://articles.latimes.com/2011/jun/21/opinion/la-oe-navarro-trade-china-20110621.

7. Ibid.

8. John Hechinger, "U.S. Teens Lag as China Soars on International Test," Bloomberg, December 7, 2010, http://www.bloomberg.com/news/2010-12-07/teens-in-u-s-rank-25th-on-math-test-trail-in-science-reading.html.

9. Andrew J. Rotherham, "Shanghai Surprise: Don't Sweat Global Test Data," *TIME*, January 20, 2011, http://www.time.com/time/nation/article/ 0,8599,2043312,00.html.

10. Anne Flaherty, "Pentagon: China's Military Power Growing," ABC News, August 16, 2010.

11. Aprille Muscara, "Wikileak Cables Reveal China's Modernising Military Might," *Global Issues*, January 13, 2011, http://www.globalissues.org/news/2011/01/13/8172.

12. Bryan Krekel, "Capability of the People's Republic of China to Conduct Cyber Warfare and Computer Network Exploitation," The US-China Economic and Security Review Commission, Northrop Grumman Corporation, October 9, 2009, 52, http://www.uscc.gov/researchpapers/2009/NorthropGrumman_PRC_Cyber_Paper_FINAL_Approved%20Report_16Oct2009.pdf.

13. Scott Robertson, "AISI calls for China currency remedy," *Metal Bulletin*, April 7, 2010.

14. Ibid.

15. Alan Tonelson, "Economic Watch: It's Time to Stop Kowtowing on Yuan Manipulation," *Washington Times*, March 30, 2010, Section A, p. 4.

16.   Patrice Hill, "Penalties sought for China over currency practices," *Washington Times*, September 16, 2010, http://www.washingtontimes.com/news/2010/sep/16/lawmakers-seek-penalties-for-china/.

17.   Chris Isidore, "How 'The Donald' could incite a trade war," CNNMoney.com, April 18, 2011, http://money.cnn.com/2011/04/17/news/economy/trump_china_trade_war/index.htm.

18.   James Bacchus, "What A Trade War With China Would Look Like," Forbes.com, February 2, 2009, http://www.forbes.com/2009/01/31/trade-wto-china-opinions-contributors_0202_james_bacchus.html.

19.   "National Income and Product Accounts Gross Domestic Product, 2nd quarter 2011 (third estimate) Corporate Profits, 2nd quarter 2011 (revised estimate)," Bureau of Economic Analysis, report released September 29, 2011, http://www.bea.gov/newsreleases/national/gdp/gdpnewsrelease.htm.

20.   "Weekly Address: President Obama: 'We Can Out-Compete Any Other Nation,'" WhiteHouse.gov, January 22, 2011, http://m.whitehouse.gov/the-press-office/2011/01/22/weekly-address-president-obama-we-can-out-compete-any-other-nation.

21.   Jamie Reno, "'Made in the USA' Makes a Comeback," NewsMax, November 2011, 23.

22.   Ibid.

23.   Ibid.

24.   James Bacchus, "What A Trade War With China Would Look Like," op. cit.

25.   Patrice Hill, "Penalties sought for China over currency practices," op. cit.

26.   Adam Smith, *Theory of Moral Sentiments* (Cambridge University Press, 2002), 95.

27.   "The Makings of a Trade War With China," *The Daily Beast*, September 27, 2010, http://www.newsweek.com/2010/09/27/the-makings-of-a-trade-war-with-china.html.

28.   Jacob Greber, "Krugman Says China Is Devaluing Its Currency, 'Stealing' Jobs," Bloomberg, October 23, 2009, http://www.bloomberg.com/apps/news?pid=news archive&sid=aUVeLdpK4Yqg.

29.   Peter Navarro, "How China unfairly bests the U.S.," op. cit.

30.   Ibid.

31.   Josh Kraushaar, "Nerves Show on Team Obama," *National Journal* Against the Grain, June 28, 2011, http://www.nationaljournal.com/columns/against-the-grain/nerves-show-on-team-obama-20110628.

32.   Government Press Release, "China to Boost Military Spending," INTERNATIONAL PRESS SERVICE, March 4, 2011, http://infoweb.newsbank.com.proxy.lib.fsu.edu/iw-search/we/InfoWeb?p_product=AWNB&p_theme=aggregated5&p_action=doc&p_docid=134C3E70680B7700&p_docnum=1&p_queryname=1.

33.   Siobhan Gorman, August Cole, and Yochi Dreazen, "Computer Spies Breach Fighter-Jet Project," *Wall Street Journal*, April 21, 2009.

34.   "Spies Breach Pentagon Fighter-Jet Project: Report," Agence France-Presse, April 21, 2009, http://infoweb.newsbank.com.proxy.lib.fsu.edu/iw-search/we/InfoWeb?p_product=AWNB&p_theme=aggregated5&p_action=doc&p_docid=127BB775B218BCD0&p_docnum=1&p_queryname=19.

35.   Krekel, "Capability of China to Conduct Cyber Warfare," op. cit., 7.

36.   Ibid., 52.

37.   Ibid.

38.   Government Press Release, "China to Boost Military Spending," op cit.

39.   Aprille Muscara, "China: Wikileak Cables Reveal China Focus on Military Upgrades," Inter Press Service English News Wire.

40.   Kelvin Wong, Nichola Saminather, and Hui-yong Yu, "The Chinese Go on a Global Homebuying Spree: Facing domestic restrictions, buyers boost markets abroad," *Bloomberg Businessweek*, June 23, 2011.

Chapter Four

1.   Ronald Reagan, *An American Life: The Autobiography* (New York: Simon & Schuster, 1990), 233.

2.   Gifts to the United States Government, U.S. Department of the Treasury, http://fms.treas.gov/faq/moretopics_gifts.html.

3.   Barbara Hollingsworth, "Virginia's 'Tax Me More Fund' is a big flop," *Washington Examiner*, March 29, 2010, http://washingtonexaminer.com/blogs/beltway-confidential/virginia-s-tax-me-more-fund-big-flop.

4.   Ronald Reagan, *An American Life: The Autobiography*, 232.

5.   Ibid., 233.

6.   "Economic Overview of Federal Tax Expenditures," Invest in Kids Working Group, The Partnership for America's Economic Success, February 20, 2007, http://www.partnershipforsuccess.org/docs/ivk/iikmeeting_slides200702weinstein.pdf.

7.   Stephen Ohlemacher, "Half of U.S. pays no federal income tax," Associated Press, April 7, 2010, available at MSNBC.com, http://www.msnbc.msn.com/id/36226444/ns/business-personal_finance/t/half-us-pays-no-federal-income-tax/.

8.   Steve Forbes and Elizabeth Ames, *How Capitalism Will Save Us: Why Free People and Free Markets Are the Best Answer to Today's Economy* (New York: Crown Business, 2009), 148.

9.   Jason Pye, "Top 1% pays more in taxes than bottom 95%," United Liberty, July 30, 2009, http://www.unitedliberty.org/articles/top-1-pays-more-in-taxes-than-bottom-95.

10.   Neil Cavuto, *Your Money or Your Life* (New York: Regan Books, 2005), 84.

11.   Steve Forbes and Elizabeth Ames, *How Capitalism Will Save Us*, 148.

12.   Ronald Reagan, *An American Life: The Autobiography*, 232.

13.   "The Dead Enders," *Wall Street Journal* Review & Outlook, December 1, 2010, http://online.wsj.com/article/SB10001424052748703326204575616843991237032.html.

14.   "What Do Corporate Income Taxes Cost American Families?" Tax Watch, Tax Foundation, http://www.taxfoundation.org/files/corporate_income_taxes_cost_families-20080818.pdf.

15.   Ronald Reagan, "Address to the Nation on the Economy," February 5, 1981, transcript available at http://www.reagan.utexas.edu/archives/speeches/ 1981/20581c.htm.

16.   "Hidden taxes you pay every day," MSN Money Central, http://articles.moneycentral.msn.com/Taxes/CutYourTaxes/HiddenTaxesYouPayEveryDay.aspx?page=2.

17.   Scott Burns, "US tax disparity may be flatter than it seems," *Boston Globe*, January 28, 2007, http://www.boston.com/business/taxes/articles/ 2007/01/28/us_tax_disparity_may_be_flatter_than_it_seems/.

18.   W. Kurt Hauser, "There's No Escaping Hauser's Law," *Wall Street Journal*, November 26, 2010, http://online.wsj.com/article/SB1000142405274870351490457560290 43209741952.html#printMode.

19.   David Brooks, "The Genteel Nation," *New York Times*, September 9, 2010, http://www.nytimes.com/2010/09/10/opinion/10brooks.html.

20.   "Night of the Living Death Tax," *Wall Street Journal* Review & Outlook, March 31, 2009, http://online.wsj.com/article/SB123846422014872229.html.

21.   Ibid.

22.   "Solutions for America: Tax Reform," Heritage Foundation, August 17, 2010, http://www.heritage.org/Research/Reports/2010/08/Tax-Reform.

23.   Adam Aigner-Treworgy, "Obama talks estate tax at final bus tour stop," CNN.com *The 1600 Report*, August 17, 2011, http://whitehouse.blogs.cnn.com/2011/08/17/obama-talks-estate-tax-at-final-bus-tour-stop/.

24.   Curtis Dubay, "The Economic Case Against the Death Tax," Heritage Foundation *The Foundry*, July 21, 2010, http://blog.heritage.org/2010/07/21/the-economic-case-against-the-death-tax/.

25.   Sam Stein, "Obama Wants Higher Capital Gains Tax Rate: Too Far Or Not Enough?" *Huffington Post*, February 26, 2009, http://www.huffingtonpost.com/2009/02/26/obama-wants-higher-capita_ n_170237.html

26.   J. D. Foster, "Obama's Capital Gains Tax Hike Unlikely to Increase Revenues," Heritage Foundation, March 24, 2010, http://www.heritage.org/Research/Reports/2010/03/Obamas-Capital-Gains-Tax-Hike-Unlikely-to-Increase-Revenues.

27.   Janet Novack, "Tax Waste: 6.1 Billion Hours Spent Complying With Federal Tax Code," Forbes, January 5, 2011, http://www.forbes.com/sites/janetnovack/2011/01/05/tax-waste-6-1-billion-hours-spent-complying-with-federal-tax-code/.

Chapter Five

1.   Quote available at Gerald R. Ford Quotes, http://www.fordlibrary museum.gov/grf/quotes.asp.

2.   Guest Writer, "The debt ceiling deal—an agreement to do nothing," MLive.com, August 4, 2011, http://www.mlive.com/opinion/grandrapids/index.ssf/2011/08/guest_commentary_debt_ceiling.html?utm_source=Justin+Amash+for+Congress+Email+List&utm_campaign=af602ae2f7-Justin_s_Editorial_on_Debt_Ceiling_8_4_2011&utm_medium=email.

3.   Stephen Ohlemacher, "Can tiny changes save Social Security?" Associated Press, May 17, 2010, available at MSNBC.com, http://www.msnbc.msn.com/id/37195779/ns/business-personal_finance/t/can-tiny-changes-save-social-security/#.TojfqLLh5Bk.

4.   Ronald Reagan "Remarks on Signing the Social Security Amendments of 1983," April 20, 1983, http://www.reagan.utexas.edu/archives/speeches/1983/42083a.htm

5.   "Sen. Rubio: 'We Don't Need New Taxes, We Need New Taxpayers,'" RealClearPolitics.com, July 7, 2011, http://www.realclearpolitics.com/video/2011/07/07/sen_rubio_we_dont_need_new_taxes_we_need_new_taxpayers.html.

6.   "Government Waste By the Numbers: Report Identifies Dozens of Overlapping Programs," FoxNews.com, March 1, 2011, http://www.foxnews.com/politics/2011/03/01/government-waste-numbers-report-identifies-dozens-duplicative-programs/.

7.   Emily Kopp, "OPM commits to stopping payments to dead people," FederalNewsRadio. com, September 23, 2011, http://www.federalnews radio.com/?nid=520&sid=2560010.

8.   "Dr. Coburn Releases New Oversight Report: 'Wastebook 2010: A Guide to Some of the Most Wasteful Government Spending of 2010,'" Tom Coburn, M.D., December 20, 2010, http://coburn.senate.gov/public/index.cfm/pressreleases?ContentRecord_ id=054487a3-ff6e-4df9-a025-48de764abe55.

9.   Edwin Mora, "U.S. Has Paid $1.44 Million for Project That is Studying the 'Social Milieu' of Male Prostitutes in Ho Chi Minh City and Hanoi," CNSNews.com, June 28, 2010, http://www.cnsnews.com/node/68628.

10. "Scores charged in massive US healthcare fraud scams," Reuters, September 8, 2011, http://in.reuters.com/article/2011/09/08/idINIndia-59213620110908.

11. "Medicare fraud strike force charges 91 individuals for approximately $295 million in false billing," HHS.gov news release, September 7, 2011, http://www.hhs.gov/ news/press/2011pres/09/20110907c.html.

12. "Medicare Fraud: A $60 Billion Crime," CBSNews.com, September 5, 2010, http:// www.cbsnews.com/stories/2009/10/23/60minutes/main5414390.shtml.

13. Sharyl Attkisson, "Federal fraud: Healthy workers took disability," CBSNews.com, February 18, 2011, http://www.cbsnews.com/stories/2011/02/18/eveningnews/ main20033639.shtml?tag=cbsnewsTwoColUpperPromoArea.

14. Tom Murse, "LIHEAP Fraud Costs Taxpayers At Least $116 Million," About.com US Government Info, November 2, 2010, http://usgovinfo.about.com/od/ moneymatters/a/LIHEAP-Outrageous-Example-of-Fraud.htm.

15. Mary Meeker, "USA Inc.: Red, White, and Very Blue," *Businessweek*, February 24, 2011, http://www.businessweek.com/magazine/content/ 11_10/b4218000828880. htm.

16. Stephen Ohlemacher, "Can tiny changes save Social Security?" Associated Press, May 17, 2010, available at MSNBC.com, http://www.msnbc.msn.com/id/37195779/ ns/business-personal_finance/t/can-tiny-changes-save-social-security/#.TojfqLL- h5Bk.

17. "Mary Meeker's Definitive Guide To The American Public Debt Crisis," *Business Insider*, http://www.businessinsider.com/mary-meeker-usa-inc-february-24-2011-2#-120.

18. "The Obama Fisc," *Wall Street Journal* Review & Outlook, January 27, 2010, http:// online.wsj.com/article/SB10001424052748703906204575027181656362948.html.

19. Victor Davis Hanson, "Obama's Spending Addiction," RealClearPolitics.com, July 28, 2011, http://www.realclearpolitics.com/articles/ 2011/07/28/obamas_spending_ addiction_110741.html.

Chapter Six

1.   George Washington, "Fifth Annual Address," December 3, 1793.

2.   David Ignatius, "Caution fills Obama's playbook," *Washington Post*, September 23, 2009, http://www.washingtonpost.com/opinions/caution-fills- obamas-playbook/2011/09/22/gIQAdNKfrK_story.html.

3.   Sam Youngman and Jordy Yager, "Obama to resume Gitmo military trials," *The Hill*, March 7, 2011, http://thehill.com/homenews/administration/147871- obama-military-commissions-to-resume-for-gitmo-detainees.

4. Editorial, "Mr. Obama's defense cuts," *Washington Post*, April 20, 2011, http://www. washingtonpost.com/opinions/mr-obamas-defense-cuts/2011/04/20/ AFlMqNEE_story.html.

5. "Defending Defense: China's Military Build-up: Implications for U.S. Defense Spending," American Enterprise Institute, Heritage Foundation, Foreign Policy Initiative, March 2011, http://www.aei.org/docLib/DefendingDefenseChina.pdf.

6. Ibid.

7. Joseph A. Bosco, "China Lobbies Washington for Arms," *Weekly Standard*, June 1, 2011, http://www.weeklystandard.com/blogs/china-lobbies-washington-arms_573140. html.

8. Dan Blumenthal and Michael Mazza, "Asia Needs a Larger U.S. Defense Budget," *Wall Street Journal*, July 5, 2011, http://online.wsj.com/article/SB10001424052702 3048031045764254140303355604.html.

9. Irwin M. Stelzer, "Our Broken China Policy," *Weekly Standard*, January 17, 2011, http://www.weeklystandard.com/articles/our-broken-china-policy_526878.html.

10. Dan Blumenthal, "China Humiliates Gates, Obama," *Weekly Standard*, January 12, 2011, http://www.weeklystandard.com/blogs/china-humiliates-gates-obama_533550.html.

11. Thomas Donnelly, "The Real Meaning of China's 'Stealth Fighter,'" *Weekly Standard*, January 13, 2011, http://www.weeklystandard.com/blogs/real-meaning-china-s-stealth-fighter_533614.html.

12. Ewen MacAskill, "WikiLeaks: Hillary Clinton's question: how can we stand up to Beijing?" *The Guardian*, December 4, 2010, http://www.guardian.co.uk/ world/2010/dec/04/wikileaks-cables-hillary-clinton-beijing.

13. Irwin M. Stelzer, "Our Broken China Policy," op. cit.

14. "Defending Defense: China's Military Build-up: Implications for U.S. Defense Spending," op. cit.

15. Julian E. Barnes and Megan K. Stack, "Russia's Putin praises Obama's missile defense decision," *Los Angeles Times*, September 19, 2009, http://articles.latimes. com/2009/sep/19/world/fg-missile-defense19.

16. Ibid.

17. "Obama: Missile defense plan not about Russia," MSNBC.com, September 20, 2009, http://www.msnbc.msn.com/id/32937784/ns/world_news-europe/t/obama-missile-defense-plan-not-about-russia/#.TpDQobLh6uI.

18. Paul Richter, "Russia pushing back on tougher sanctions against Iran," *Los Angeles Times*, September 24, 2010, http://articles.latimes.com/2010/sep/24/world/ la-fg-russia-sanctions-20100925.

19. Daniel Halper, "U.S. Intelligence Confirms: Russia Bombed U.S. Embassy," op. cit.

20. Graham Allison, "Obama should test Iran's nuclear offer," *Washington Post*, October 6, 2011, http://www.washingtonpost.com/opinions/obama-should-test-irans-nuclear-offer/2011/10/06/gIQAdAmDRL_story.html.

21. Jay Solomon, "Iran Rejects Proposed U.S. Military Hot Line," *Wall Street Journal*, October 4, 2011, http://online.wsj.com/article/SB100014240529702037919045766 09093178338996.html.

22. Trita Parsi, "Iran's growing bluster spells danger," *Los Angeles Times*, October 2, 2011, http://articles.latimes.com/2011/oct/02/opinion/la-oe-parsi-iran-20111002.

23. Jay Solomon, "Iran Rejects Proposed U.S. Military Hot Line," op. cit.
24. Ibid.
25. William J. Broad, John Markoff, and David E. Sanger, "Israeli Test on Worm Called Crucial in Iran Nuclear Dely," *New York Times*, January 15, 2011, http://www.nytimes.com/2011/01/16/world/middleeast/16stuxnet.html?page wanted=all.
26. David E. Sanger, "Iran Moves to Shelter Its Nuclear Fuel Program," *New York Times*, September 1, 2011, http://www.nytimes.com/2011/09/02/world/middleeast/02iran.html.
27. See "Obama: Iran Doesn't Pose a Threat...Iran is a Grave Threat," posted on YouTube.com, May 20, 2008, http://www.youtube.com/watch?v= vaG6s05MKeM.
28. Sara A. Carter, "U.S. confirms attacks by Pakistani military units," *Washington Examiner*, October 2, 2011, http://washingtonexaminer.com/politics/2011/10/us-confirms-attacks-pakistani-military-units.
29. Max Boot, "Frenemies in Pakistan," *Weekly Standard*, October 10, 2011, http://www.weeklystandard.com/articles/frenemies-pakistan_594669.html.
30. Sara A. Carter, "U.S. confirms attacks by Pakistani military units," op. cit.
31. Max Boot, "Frenemies in Pakistan," op. cit.
32. Neil Munro, "Free for all: Up to 20,000 anti-aircraft missiles stolen in Libya," *Daily Caller*, September 27, 2011, http://dailycaller.com/2011/09/27/free-for-all-up-to-20000-anti-aircraft-missiles-stolen-in-libya/.
33. Brian Ross and Matthew Cole, "Nightmare in Libya: Thousands of Surface-to-Air Missiles Unaccounted for," ABCNews.com, September 27, 2011, http://abcnews.go.com/Blotter/nightmare-libya-20000-surface- air-missiles-missing/story?id=14610199.
34. Neil Munro, "Free for all: Up to 20,000 anti-aircraft missiles stolen in Libya," op. cit.
35. "Iran 'discreetly aided Libyan rebels,'" AFP, August 28, 2011, http://www.google.com/hostednews/afp/article/ALeqM5jj6m9cMuH8ZXj5AgMQLjLVHFDhlA?doCId=CNG.9b666507647200654b641466e2317b3d.501.

Chapter Seven

1. Katherine Bradley, "Confronting the Unsustainable Growth of Welfare Entitlements: Principles of Reform and the Next Steps," Heritage Foundation *Backgrounder* #2427, June 24, 2010, http://www.heritage.org/research/reports/2010/06/confronting-the-unsustainable-growth-of-welfare-entitlements-principles-of-reform-and-the-next-steps.
2. Ed Feulner, "A better way to reform welfare," *Washington Times*, April 5, 2011, http://www.washingtontimes.com/news/2011/apr/5/a-better- way-to-reform-welfare/.
3. Katherine Bradley, "Confronting the Unsustainable Growth of Welfare Entitlements: Principles of Reform and the Next Steps," op. cit.
4. Jack Dolan, "Welfare recipients get $12,000 from strip club ATMs," *Los Angeles Times*, July 1, 2010, http://articles.latimes.com/2010/jul/01/local/la-me-welfare-20100701.
5. Mark Weaver, "FFX Subsidized Housing Tenants Live Large On Your Dime," WMAL.com, http://www.wmal.com/Article.asp?id=2225336.
6. Dinesh D'Souza, "10 Great Things," National Review Online, July 2, 2003, http://www.nationalreview.com/articles/207396/10-great-things-dinesh-dsouza.

7.   Robert Rector and Rachel Sheffield, "Understanding Poverty in the United States: Surprising Facts About America's Poor," Heritage Foundation *Backgrounder* #2607, September 13, 2011, http://www.heritage.org/research/reports/2011/09/understanding-poverty-in-the-united-states-surprising-facts-about-americas-poor.

8.   Ibid.

9.   Robert Rector, "How Poor Are America's Poor? Examining the 'Plague' of Poverty in America," Heritage Foundation *Backgrounder* #2604, http://www.heritage.org/research/reports/2007/08/how-poor-are-americas-poor-examining-the-plague-of-poverty-in- america.

10.   "The Father Factor," National Fatherhood Initiative, http://www.fatherhood.org/media/consequences-of-father-absence-statistics.

11.   Information formerly available at http://beta2.tbo.com/news/opinion/2008/apr/04/pa-the-welfare-system-needs-an-exit-plan-ar-132691/.

12.   Robert Rector, "Marriage: America's Greatest Weapon Against Child Poverty," Heritage Foundation *Backgrounder* #2465, September 16, 2010, http://www.heritage.org/research/reports/2010/09/marriage-america-s-greatest-weapon-against-child-poverty.

13.   Katherine Bradley, "Confronting the Unsustainable Growth of Welfare Entitlements: Principles of Reform and the Next Steps," op. cit.

14.   Ibid.

15.   Ibid.

16.   Ed Feulner, "A Better Way to Reform Welfare," *Washington Times*, April 5, 2011, http://www.washingtontimes.com/news/2011/apr/5/a-better-way-to-reform-welfare/.

17.   Robert Rector and Rachel Sheffield, "Understanding Poverty in the United States: Surprising Facts About America's Poor," op. cit.

18.   James Bovard, "The Food-Stamp Crime Wave," *Wall Street Journal*, June 23, 2011, http://online.wsj.com/article/SB10001424052702304657804576401412033504294.html.

19.   Ibid.

20.   Ibid.

21.   Ibid.

22.   Jason Stein, "State takes 1,200 Milwaukee County inmates off FoodShare," JSOnline.com, September 24, 2011, http://www.jsonline.com/watchdog/130511318.html.

23.   Dawson Bell, "Michigan wants lotto winner off food stamps," *USA Today*, May 19, 2011, http://www.usatoday.com/news/nation/2011-05-19-lottery-winner-food-stamps_n.htm.

24.   Scott Shifrel, "$8 million food stamp fraud mastermind pleads guilty to scam," New York Daily News, August 10, 2011, http://articles.nydailynews.com/2011-08-10/news/29890597_1_food-stamp-mail-fraud-guilty-plea.

25.   Craig Schneider and Tammy Joyner, "Housing crisis reaches full boil in East Point; 62 injured," AJC.com, August 11, 2010, http://www.ajc.com/news/atlanta/housing-crisis-reaches-full-589653.html.

26.   Katherine Bradley, "Confronting the Unsustainable Growth of Welfare Entitlements: Principles of Reform and the Next Steps," op. cit.

27.   Robert Rector and Rachel Sheffield, "Understanding Poverty in the United States: Surprising Facts About America's Poor," op. cit.

28.   "A Sad Day for Poor Children," *New York Times*, August 1, 1996.

29.   Ed Feulner, "A Better Way to Reform Welfare," op. cit.

30. Ibid.

31. "The Welfare Reform Act of 2011," RSC, http://rsc.jordan.house.gov/Solutions/
wra.htm; and Katherine Bradley, "Picking Up Where '96 Welfare Reform Left Off,"
National Review Online, March 17, 2011, http://www.nationalreview.com/blogs/
print/262372.

32. "H.R. 1167: Welfare Reform Act of 2011," Republican Study Committee, March
2011, http://rsc.jordan.house.gov/UploadedFiles/Summary_WelfareReformAct.
pdf.

33. Michael Peltier, "Florida to test all welfare recipients for drugs," Reuters, May
31, 2011, http://www.reuters.com/article/2011/05/31/us-florida-welfare-
drugs-idUSTRE74U6W320110531.

34. Ibid.

35. "Florida government defends requiring drug tests for welfare recipients," CNN News
Blogs, June 5, 2011, http://news.blogs.cnn.com/2011/06/05/florida-government-defends-
requiring-drug-tests-for-welfare-recipients/.

36. Michael Peltier, "Florida to test all welfare recipients for drugs," op. cit.

Chapter Eight

1. Lydia Saad, "Cost Is Foremost Healthcare Issue for Americans," Gallup, September
23, 2009, http://www.gallup.com/poll/123149/cost-is-foremost-healthcare-issue-
for-americans.aspx.

2. Melissa Allison, "Starbucks CEO Howard Schultz discusses turnaround," *Seattle Times*,
March 12, 2011, http://seattletimes.nwsource.com/html/businesstechnology/2014461881_
starbucks13.html.

3. "Great Suppression II," UBS, September 19, 2011, http://coburn.senate.gov/public/
index.cfm?a=Files.Serve&File_id=c968aed0-e358-451b-9f68-c98078f75156.

4. Ibid.

5. Sally Pipes, "The Best Jobs Program? Full Repeal Of ObamaCare," Forbes, September 19, 2011, http://www.forbes.com/sites/sallypipes/2011/09/19/the-best-jobs-
program-full-repeal-of-obamacare/.

6. Sam Baker, "HHS grants 106 new healthcare waivers," *The Hill* Healthwatch, August
19, 2011, http://thehill.com/blogs/healthwatch/health-reform-implementation/
177581-hhs-grants-106-new-healthcare-waivers.

7. Milton R. Wolf, "Obamacare waiver corruption must stop," *Washington Times*, May
20, 2011, http://www.washingtontimes.com/news/2011/may/20/obamacare-waiver-
corruption-must-stop/.

8. Grace-Marie Turner, James C. Capretta, Thomas P. Miller, and Robert E. Moffit,
Why Obamacare is Wrong for America (New York: Broadside, 2011), 45.

9. Julian Pecquet and Sam Baker, "Spotlight back on healthcare law," *The Hill*
Healthwatch, September 27, 2011, http://thehill.com/blogs/healthwatch/
health-reform-implementation/184293-spotlight-back-onto-health-law.

10. John Merline, "ObamaCare's Growing List Of Broken Promises," Investors.com,
October 5, 2011, http://www.investors.com/NewsAndAnalysis/Article/587194/
201110051841/ObamaCares-Broken-Promises.aspx.

11. Robert J. Samuelson, "Stuck in a vicious health-care cost circle," *Washington Post*,
September 29, 2011, http://www.washingtonpost.com/blogs/post-partisan/post/
stuck-in-a-vicious-health-care-cost-circle/2011/09/29/gIQAPoFd7K_blog.html.

12. "Health Reform Will Create 400,000 Jobs 'Almost Immediately,'" ReaClearPolitics. com, February 25, 2010, http://www.realclearpolitics.com/video/2010/02/25/ pelosi_health_reform_will_create_400000_jobs_almost_immediately.html.

13. Grace-Marie Turner, "ObamaCare's job-killing impact is just getting started," *Chicago Tribune*, April 1, 2010, http://articles.chicagotribune.com/2010-04-01/ news/ct-oped-0402-business-20100401_1_drug-benefits-drug-program-tax-change.

14. Examiner Editorial, "Obamacare would hurt small business," *Washington Examiner*, July 12, 2009, http://washingtonexaminer.com/editorials/2009/07/obam-acare-would-hurt-small-business.

15. Sally Pipes, "The Best Jobs Program? Full Repeal Of ObamaCare," op. cit.

16. J. Lester Feder & Kate Nocera, "CBO: Health law to shrink workforce by 800,000," *Politico*, February 10, 2011, http://www.politico.com/news/stories/0211/49273. html.

17. Kathryn Nix, "House Education and Workforce Committee: Obamacare Is a Job Killer," Heritage Foundation *The Foundry*, February 17, 2011, http://blog.heritage. org/2011/02/17/house-education-and-workforce-committee-obamacare-is-a-job-killer/.

18. John Merline, "ObamaCare's Growing List Of Broken Promises," op. cit.

19. Marissa Cevallos, "One in three employers may drop health benefits, report says," *Los Angeles Times*, June 7, 2011, http://articles.latimes.com/2011/jun/07/news/la-heb-healthcare-employer-20110607.

20. Examiner Editorial, "Scary truth about Obamacare keeps seeping out," *Washington Examiner*, September 25, 2011, http://washingtonexaminer.com/opin-ion/2011/09/scary-truth-about-obamacare-keeps-seeping-out.

21. Jeffrey H. Anderson, "CBO: Obamacare Would Cost Over $2 Trillion," *Weekly Standard*, March 18, 2010, http://www.weeklystandard.com/print/blogs/cbo-obamacare-would-cost-over-2-trillion.

22. Editorial, "The Uninsured," *New York Times*, August 22, 2009, http://www.nytimes. com/2009/08/23/opinion/23sun1.html?pagewanted=print.

23. Betsy McCaughey, *Obama Health Law: What It Says And How to Overturn It* (New York: Encounter Books, 2010), 15.

24. Ibid., 50.

25. The Honorable Tom Feeney, "Interstate Competition and Choice in Health Insurance: The American Way," Heritage Foundation *Backgrounder* #2386, March 16, 2010, http://www.heritage.org/research/reports/2010/03/interstate-competition-and-choice-in-health-insurance- the-american-way.

26. Review & Outlook, "The Competition Cure," *Wall Street Journal*, August 23, 2009, http://online.wsj.com/article/SB10001424052970203550604574360923109310680. html.

27. Ed Moirressey, "Tort reform the key to cutting health-care costs?" HotAir.com, July 30, 2009, http://hotair.com/archives/2009/07/30/tort-reform-the-key-to-cutting-health-care-costs/.

28. Ibid.

29. Jim Angle, "GOP-Proposed Tort Reform Would Reduce Health Care Costs, Analysts Say," FoxNews.com, March 3, 2010, http://www.foxnews.com/politics/2010/03/03/gop-proposed-tort-reform-reduce-health-care-costs-analysts-say/.

Chapter Nine

1. "Border States Deal With more Illegal Immigrant Crime Than Most, Data Suggest," FoxNews.com, April 30, 2010, http://www.foxnews.com/politics/2010/04/29/border-states-dealing-illegal-immigrant-crime-data-suggests/.
2. Jack Martin and Eric Ruark, "The Fiscal Burden of Illegal Immigration on United States Taxpayers," Federation for American Immigration Reform (FAIR), July 2010 (rev. February 2011), http://www.fairus.org/site/DocServer/USCostStudy_2010.pdf?docID=4921.
3. "Criminal Alien Statistics: Information on Incarcerations, Arrests, and Costs," United States Government Accountability Office Report to Congressional Requesters, March 2011, http://www.gao.gov/new.items/d11187.pdf.
4. Solomon Moore, "Study Shows Sharp Rise in Latino Federal Convicts," *New York Times*, February 18, 2009, http://www.nytimes.com/2009/02/19/us/19immig.html.
5. Ibid.
6. Terence P. Jeffrey, "Justice Department: Border Patrol Agents Assaulted Daily, Kidnappings Every 35 Hours in Phoenix, 1 in 5 Teens Using Drugs Predominantly Supplied by Mexican Traffickers," CNSNews.com, April 28, 2010, http://www.cnsnews.com/node/64910.
7. "Al Qaeda seeks tie to local gangs," *Washington Times*, September 28, 2004, http://www.washingtontimes.com/news/2004/sep/28/20040928-123346-3928r/.
8. Jana Winter, "Feds Issue Terror Watch for the Texas/Mexico Border," FoxNews.com, May 26, 2010, http://www.foxnews.com/us/2010/05/26/terror-alert-mexican-border/.
9. Ray Walser, Ph.D., Jena Baker McNeill, and Jessica Zuckerman, "The Human Tragedy of Illegal Immigration: Greater Efforts Needed to Combat Smuggling and Violence," Heritage Foundation *Backgrounder* #2568, June 22, 2011, http://www.heritage.org/Research/Reports/2011/06/The-Human-Tragedy-of-Illegal-Immigration-Greater-Efforts-Needed-to-Combat-Smuggling-and-Violence.
10. Caroline Black, "Illegal Immigrant Carlos Montano Charged with Killing Nun in Drunk Driving Crash," CBSNews.com, August 4, 2010, http://www.cbsnews.com/2102-504083_162-20012650.html?tag=contentMain;contentBody.
11. Jack Martin and Eric Ruark, "The Fiscal Burden of Illegal Immigration on United States Taxpayers," op. cit.
12. "Study: 70% of Texas' illegal immigrant families receive welfare," Chron.com, http://blog.chron.com/txpotomac/2011/04/study-70-of-texas-illegal immigrant-families-receive-welfare/.
13. "Welfare Tab for Children of Illegal Immigrants Estimated at $600M in L.A. County," FoxNews.com, January 19, 2011, http://www.foxnews.com/politics/2011/01/19/welfare-tab-children-illegal-immi grants-estimated-m-la-county/.

14. "The Debate Over 'Anchor Babies' And Citizenship," NPR *Talk of the Nation*, http://www.npr.org/templates/story/story.php?storyId=129279863.

15. Nell Henderson, "Effect of Immigration on Jobs, Wages Is Difficult for Economists to Nail Down," *Washington Post*, April 15, 2006, http://www.washing tonpost.com/wp-dyn/content/article/2006/04/14/AR2006041401686.html.

16. Ibid.

17. Charles Kadlec, "The Great African-American Depression," Forbes, September 6, 2011, http://www.forbes.com/sites/charleskadlec/2011/09/06/the-great-african-american-depression/.

18. David Jackson, "Obama's line about alligators on the border draws fire," *USA Today*, May 14, 2011, http://content.usatoday.com/communities/theoval/post/2011/05/obamas-line-about-alligators-on-the-border-draws-fire/1.

19. "Mexico Sees Record Drop in Remittances," Associated Press, January 27, 2010, available at CBSNews.com, http://www.cbsnews.com/stories/ 2010/01/27/world/main6148649.shtml.

20. "Merit-based Permanent Immigration: A Look at Canada's Point System," Senate Republican Policy Committee, May 22, 2007, http://rpc.senate.gov/public/_files/052207MeritBasedImmigLookatCanadaPoint SystemLB.pdf.

21. "The United States v Canada," The Economist Democracy in America blog, May 20, 2011, http://www.economist.com/blogs/democracyin america /2011/05/immigration.

22. "Merit-based Permanent Immigration: A Look at Canada's Point System," Senate Republican Policy Committee, op. cit.

23. Daniel B. Wood, "Where U.S.-Mexico border fence is tall, border crossings fall," *Christian Science Monitor*, April 1, 2008, http://www.csmonitor.com/USA/2008/0401/p01s05-usgn.html.

24. Ibid.

25. David B. Rivkin Jr. and Lee A. Casey, "Obama's illegal move on immigration," *Washington Post*, September 2, 2011, http://www.washingtonpost.com/opinions/obamas-illegal-move-on-immigration/2011/09/01/gIQATKQexJ_story.html.

26. James R. Edwards, Jr., "Obama's Backdoor Amnesty for 300,000 Immigrants," *Human Events*, September 12, 2011, http://www.humanevents.com/article.php?print=yes&id=46102.

27. Ibid.

28. Amy Woods, "Rep. King Upset With Amnesty for Obama Uncle," NewsMax.com, September 10, 2011, http://www.newsmax.com/InsideCover/RepKing-Upset-Amnesty-ObamaUncle/2011/09/10/id/410436.

29. Hans von Spakovsky, "Pampering Illegals, Endangering Americans: The Obama Administration's Immigration Policy," Heritage Foundation The Foundry, August 9, 2010, http://blog.heritage.org/2010/08/09/pampering-illegals-endangering-americans-the-obama-administration%E2%80%99s-immigration-policy/. See also, *www.iceunion.org/download/250 cca-pbnds-letter.pdf.*

Chapter Ten

1. Catherine Rampell, "Many With New College Degree Find the Job Market Humbling," *New York Times*, May 18, 2011, http://www.nytimes.com/2011/05/19/business/economy/19grads.html?_r=1.
2. Associated Press, "Americans give record $295B to charity," *USA Today*, June 25, 2007, http://www.usatoday.com/news/nation/2007-06-25-charitable_N.htm.

Afterword

1. L. Gordon Crovitz, "Steve Jobs's Advice for Obama," *Wall Street Journal*, October 31, 2011, http://online.wsj.com/article/SB100014240529702036875045770037636 59779448.html.
2. X-PRIZE Foundation's official website, see "Who we are" in the "About" section, http://www.xprize.org/about/who-we-are.

INDEX

natural gas and, 15, 23–24
as number one, 2, 4, 190
offshore drilling and, 26
power of, 27, 70, 72, 94, 107, 190
wealth of, 7–8, 16, 19, 27, 70, 75, 107, 156
United States president
as commander in chief, 4, 7, 86, 89
as dealmaker, 4–5, 73
jobs and, 4, 8

V
Van Susteren, Greta, 170
Variety, 166
Venezuela, 19, 20, 86, 99
ViVe TV, 20
Voice, The, 174

W
Wall Street, 40
Wall Street Journal, 14, 44, 61, 80, 92, 97, 113
Walmart, 31, 110
Washington Post, 18, 52, 142, 159
Washington, George, 85
Watters, Jesse, 169
Weiner, Anthony, 164–65
welfare
food stamp crime, 113–14

food stamps, 3, 113–15, 157
fraud and, 69, 70, 76–77, 83, 106, 113–14, 118
luxury subsidized housing, 106
Medicaid, 50, 68, 70, 82, 111, 112, 129
Medicare, 50, 68, 69–70, 76–77, 78, 82–83
Social Security, 50, 68–70, 77, 79–80, 82–83, 111, 145
Welfare Reform Act of 1996, 115–17
Welfare Reform Act of 2011, 116
Weymouth, Lally, 159, 161
Wharton School of Business, 3
Wharton School of Finance, 186
White, Susan, 38
White House Correspondents' Dinner, 159–161
Williams, Brian, 167
Wilson, Cecil, 133
Wintour, Anna, 161
Wolf, Frank, 39
Wright, Bob, 166

X
X-PRIZE Foundation, 190

Z
Zubin, Robert, 21
Zucker, Jeff, 166, 172